All Hands on Deck

All Hands on Deck

*Choosing the Right People
for the Right Jobs*

RICHARD WARNER

THE ARMARIUM PRESS INC.
NEW IPSWICH, NEW HAMPSHIRE

Festina lente and the crab and butterfly woodcut are registered trademarks of The Armarium Press Inc. on file with the U.S. Patent and Trademark Office. All other brand and product names used in this book are trade names, service marks, trademarks, or registered trademarks of their respective owners.

Printing History
2 4 6 8 10 9 7 5 3
First Edition
Copyright © 2006 by Richard Warner

All rights reserved.

No part of this book may be reproduced or transmitted in any form or by any means, electronic or mechanical, including photocopying, recording, or by any information storage and retrieval system, Internet-based or otherwise, without prior written permission from The Armarium Press, except for brief quotations used in a review.

ISBN-13: 978-09707825-4-0
ISBN: 09707825-4-3

Illustrations copyright © 2006 by John Clarke.
Crab and butterfly woodcut by Matthew Grogan.
Book design by Christyann Rothmel.

Printed in the United States of America.

THE ARMARIUM PRESS.
110 MOUNTAIN VIEW DRIVE
NEW IPSWICH, NEW HAMPSHIRE 03071
www.TheArmariumPress.com

ACKNOWLEDGMENTS

First of all, I wish to thank my wife, Mary Pat. Without your support and encouragement, I would never have been able to start Warner Design Associates. Your ability to listen to my fears and dreams, your counsel when I was anxious, and your steady demeanor all supported me when I needed it. I not only want to dedicate this book to you, I want to dedicate my career to you. Certainly without you, they never would have happened. You are truly the greatest blessing in my life.

I want to thank God for the inspiration for this book. The theme and the structure appeared to me one morning while I was getting ready for work. I truly feel the ideas were born of divine inspiration and are a gift from God. Thank you, Lord, for the words that were produced on paper.

I also want to thank my son, Scott, and daughter, Blair. As I witnessed your hard work at school and dedication to your futures, I became more conscientious about my own career. You both are inspirations to me, and I'm blessed to be your dad.

Finally, I want to thank my own father, Bob Warner. You allowed me to be an art major in college, even though you thought it was some crazy-ass idea. It wasn't the path you had picked out for me, but you supported my decision to create my own destiny. Thank you, Dad, for the freedom to live my own life.

For my beloved wife, Mary Pat

TABLE OF CONTENTS

Chapter 1	Life on Board	11
Chapter 2	The Explorer	19
Chapter 3	The Navigator	31
Chapter 4	The Captain	41
Chapter 5	The First Mate	51
Chapter 6	The Crew Member	63
Chapter 7	The Stowaway	75
Chapter 8	Assembling Your Crew	87
Chapter 9	Mutiny at Sea	103
Chapter 10	Land Ho!	113
Index		121

CHAPTER ONE

Life on Board

Scalawags, the lot of 'em! How else must the sea-faring explorers of old have described their crews – assembled as they were by royal edicts to empty out the prisons? You think you're setting off on a nice, quiet trip to discover a new way to the Spice Islands, and you learn you've got a handful of thieves, murderers, and random ne'er-do-wells in the hull. Isn't it enough that you've got to deal with the rising cost of tar and the threat of competition from the French *and* the Portuguese?

Renaissance explorers or 21st-century entrepreneurs, no one goes into business to deal with people problems. You choose a field because you have experience with it, or it's a family tradition, or it promises money, fame, or independence. But as your venture grows, you will be forced to deal with difficult people and sticky situations. Sooner or later, we all find ourselves in HR Hell.

You didn't sign up for these headaches – so what do you do now? Probably the biggest mental hurdle every business owner and manager must overcome is accepting that *your employees are not all like you.* If they were, don't you think they'd be launching their own businesses and fighting you for customers?! Take this knowledge to heart, and suddenly all those nagging questions that keep you awake at night are a little less mystifying. "I'm happy, so why isn't my staff?" "Why can't they just do things the right way?" "Will a pay raise fix the morale problem?" "Last week was great, so why did this one fall apart?" "Is this a business, or a counseling center?!"

Much like Americans abroad who think speaking English loudly will help foreigners understand them, managers who assume their employees possess the same values and attitudes they do miss the point. The problem is not the volume; it's the language. Effective management begins with understanding what each person who works for you is looking for from the job.

How often do we see managers assigning people to positions or projects for which they're unsuited?

I once ran roughshod over problems and people, creating more havoc than help among the staff of my marketing design firm. I blindly patched up conflicts with bandages when I should have rushed into surgery. I leapt in with scalpels when three minutes of listening would have cured the trouble. I lost talented, dependable employees because I lacked formal HR training and inconsistently applied the "people skills" I did possess. I kept destructive workers around too long because I just wasn't paying attention.

Like many small-business owners, I was too busy running my company to spend time learning how to run it better. In the school of hard knocks, I had a brutal teacher, but the lessons of experience did begin to sink in gradually.

And then, one day, I realized a method was emerging from my management madness....

Perhaps it's the result of a life spent near the ocean, but I've found that a nautical analogy is a useful tool for identifying and managing workplace personality types.

Imagine that each project or set of goals your business undertakes is like loading a ship with cargo, sailing to some distant land, and delivering the goods. Shouldn't be too difficult – if your ship is a rowboat, the cargo a picnic lunch, and your distant land but a few hundred yards across the lake.

If your ship is a large freighter, your destination port lies across the ocean, and the goods in your cargo hold are perishable, the task is much more difficult. You'd better have someone capable at the helm, a navigator for guidance, an engineer to keep the engine running, a cook to feed the crew, and deck hands to do everything else. No crew? Your ship won't go far. Deck hand doing the navigating? You'll never make it to port.

It sounds so simple. Choose the right people for the right jobs, and you're sure to enjoy a calm and profitable journey. Yet how often do we see managers assigning people to positions or projects for which they're completely unsuited? Such attempts meet with as much success as using a saw to pound nails and a hammer to tighten bolts. Or, to keep up the nautical theme, forcing an anchor to adjust the tiller and a compass to gauge wind direction.

Inevitably, the result is a mess: The manager gets angry that the "anchors" aren't doing a good job. Conflict arises, and communication breaks down. The "anchors" quit, or are fired. Exasperated, the manager hires a "boat hook" to do the work of a "shackle" only to experience more failure. Sometimes, by dumb luck, he hires a "winch" to help raise the sails. Emboldened with success, he runs off and hires a bunch of "winches," soon to discover the new "winches" aren't very good for swabbing decks.

If the results are so predictable, why can't managers break free of this cycle? Well, it's not so easy identifying people when they themselves often don't know who they are! Sure, most folks can provide a superficial description: education, interests, training, job history, et cetera.

When it comes to goals and aspirations, however, most people really haven't thought their feelings through completely. Many were channeled into career tracks by school counselors, parents, or friends, rather than letting their own interests and talents fuel a conscious decision. Some are hung up on previous failures at work, while others find themselves stuck in a certain job just to pay the rent. Very few of us are blessed with a mentor who truly understands us and can guide us to our "perfect" career.

The result is that prospective employees come to the job interview wearing all kinds of disguises. They lug the baggage of hidden motivations and what are often conflicting long- and short-term goals. They present themselves as the people they think you want to hire, rather than flying under their true colors and asking whether they are the right fit for the job.

Still, you have an opening to fill on your crew, and the new applicant seems qualified. You strike a deal and welcome him aboard. You introduce him to his shipmates, show him his quarters, and explain his duties. Smooth sailing, right? If only life on board were always so easy....

After you shove off, you might begin to hear low rumblings of trouble. If the new worker is a cook, perhaps the toast is always burnt. If he's an engineer, mysterious sounds and smoke belch from below deck. And that new deck hand? Well, someone caught him fast asleep in the cargo hold. The smart manager knows he must deal swiftly with such problems before they get out of hand: Provide some mentoring from a senior cook, an operating manual for the new engineer, and a little chat about responsibility for the deck hand. Teaching the engineer how to make toast won't help, nor will handing an engine manual to the deck hand.

> **Teaching the engineer how to make toast won't help, nor will handing an engine manual to the deck hand.**

Of course, what helps one cook doesn't always help another. The necessary "fix" is often a unique solution for a unique individual. Yet it does help you navigate these choppy waters if you know what general type of person each of your employees is....

So, let's meet the six characters who staff our ship of commerce: the Explorer, the Navigator, the Captain, the First Mate, the Crew Member, and the Stowaway.

As you get to know this seaworthy crew in the following pages, keep in mind that they are "purebreds," the archetype of each personality. Out in the real world, people aren't usually 100 percent Explorer or Captain or First Mate. (Haven't we all worked with someone who seemed like a 100-percent Stowaway though?) Most folks are a combination of more than one of these personalities, a combination that may change with age, experience, or circumstance. But there's probably one type that is most commonly "us" when at work. This general personality is the one your boss, co-workers, and subordinates deal with.

You'll find that my nautical analogy applies whether you manage five or 500 workers, and whether your ship of commerce is a lone craft or just one ship within an entire corporate fleet. Every department has its own Captain, after all, and while not every small- or medium-sized business has all six nautical characters on board at any given time, most need each type (except the Stowaway!) at some point in the company's growth.

> **I had much to learn, but I'd charted a new course and pushed free of the moorings. Anchors aweigh!**

Before we cast off, a few words of introduction about your guide on this high seas adventure....

* * *

My own story is one of a reluctant businessman. No M.B.A. or degree in finance for me.... I applied to San Diego State University to study art so I'd have plenty of time for my true avocation: surfing. Diploma in hand four years later, I faced the question that's plagued millions of liberal arts majors before me: What to do? What to *do?!*

So, I became a high school art teacher, following in the footsteps of older friends who convinced me that a job in which you worked fewer than 180 days a year made for one sweet career plan. Little did I know! After seven years of surprises (I'm supposed to *parent* my 175 students, too?), frustration, and eventually boredom and depression, I wanted out.

With the unwavering support of my fabulous wife, Mary Pat, I embarked on a new career. A photographer friend introduced me to several potential clients, and I soon had my first freelance assignment as a graphic designer. Well aware I knew nothing about the real-world aspects of what I'd studied in school, I dusted off my college credentials and got to work. Talking to printers, typesetters, illustrators, photographers – anyone I could – I soaked up every bit of advice and inside information like a sponge.

I felt like a kid on Christmas morning the day I finished that first assignment! The thrill of accomplishing something on my very own... the excitement of helping a client move one step closer to his own business goals... how cool! I knew I had much to learn, but I had charted a new course and pushed free of the moorings. Anchors aweigh!

Thirty years later, Warner Design Associates enjoys a client roster that includes Callaway Golf and Chevrolet, General Nutrition Centers and MGM Mirage, Sony and the San Diego Zoo, as well as countless small businesses. Major corporation or fledgling entrepreneur, the creative process is the same: *What are we selling? Who is the intended audience? What is the competition up to? What's our timeline? What's the budget? How will we measure success?* And we must roll all these constraints into the creative process if we are to meet the client's goal. Add to the process the interesting and often conflicting personalities involved, and each new project becomes a fun and truly challenging puzzle.

The opportunity to immerse myself in my clients' businesses has been a surprising bonus. I've explored the inner workings of the apparel, fitness, toy, education, entertainment, cosmetics, gaming, sporting goods, medical, automotive, banking, real estate, furniture, travel, and electronics industries. I've been able to pretend I'm a heart surgeon and a casino owner, a retail tycoon and a software engineer. I've shared in their frustrations and challenges and learned what makes their businesses tick.

I've hit my share of rough patches along the way, and you'll read about plenty of my management "challenges" in the following pages. We all have those days when it feels like you're doing nothing but bailing water like crazy. As long as your ship of commerce is still afloat after a storm passes, there's cause for comfort. Those very experiences serve to fine-tune our seamanship skills and make us better managers in the long run.

I don't hit the waves as much as I did when I was in college. (How many of us in our late 50s still do what we did at 20 anyway?) But I've been blessed with a great career in a dynamic field that offers continual opportunities for learning. Who would have thought this San Diego surfer dude would end up with a "real job," running a real company? This crazy world sure has been good to me.

So, welcome aboard! I hope you packed your Dramamine, because things could get a little rocky for the next 100-some pages. The realization you might have Stowaways in the hold and no Captain at the helm is enough to make anyone queasy. As you get your sea legs, though, I am confident you'll gain a perspective that will pay off for many successful voyages in the future.

CHAPTER TWO

The Explorer

What would our world be without Explorers? A great deal smaller, certainly. Explorers push the boundaries of geography, and of imagination. Explorers challenge the frontiers of possibility: The world isn't flat? Man will never fly? Customers won't pay a premium for overnight mail delivery? "Not so!" said the Explorers, as they dragged the naysayers into the future.

Explorers don't recognize the "shoulds" of the world. Most of us operate within a set of guidelines acquired from our parents, our friends, our culture, and our country. Do well in school, go to college, get a job.... Follow mom or dad's footsteps into a family business or career.... These paths serve many of us well.

The Explorers acknowledge these conventional courses early on in life, and then set sail in a completely different direction. Newness and novelty thrill them. Like the sailors of old who kept going even where the maps read "Beyond this be dragons," Explorers feel most alive when facing the unknown.

The rest of us keep our eyes on these Explorers (and sometimes even chuckle with glee when they fail). Yet we secretly admire these brave characters' thirst for adventure and the ease with which they embrace risk. Fear is never an Explorer's first response to change, challenge, or uncharted seas. Explorers see possibilities the rest of us cannot even imagine. Without Explorers raising our eyes to the horizon, and to the stars, our ships would never leave port.

Explorers in the business world are no different. They take chances and maintain a steady course even in the face of setbacks. Afraid of failure? Not Explorers! The risk is just part of the adventure. Ever on the lookout for new customers, better products or services, and increased profits, Explorers regard a company's past as just that: *past*. "What's next?" is their rallying cry. Explorers see not what a business is, but what it can become.

Most people don't remember that it was Magellan's ship that made it. Magellan the man did not.

Sounds great, you're thinking to yourself. So, why not go out and hire a boat full of Explorers? Because the result would be as chaotic as a kitchen full of cooks. Explorers are leaders, not followers. In the end, they love the idea more than the event. The spirit of a truly visionary Explorer can inspire his crew to reach safe port even when he himself is long gone.

Consider Ferdinand Magellan of Portugal. History credits him with the first circumnavigation of the world. What most people don't remember is that it was Magellan's ship that made it. Magellan the man did not. A little more than halfway around the world, he lost his life in the Philippine

Islands in a battle with local tribes. In fact, only one of Magellan's five ships completed the historic sea voyage. The other four vessels were lost in storms, abandoned along the journey, or seized by foreign powers. Of the 241 people who left dock with Magellan, only 18 returned three years later. Illness, mutiny, violence, and accidents claimed the rest.

When you have Explorers on your ship, you'll get lots of ideas, lots of activity, and you might lose your life in the Philippines! Explorers are not tidy. Zooming around like madmen, they often forget to work out the details from A to Z and can be careless with business protocol. Yet they can be great visionaries and inspire those around them to achieve great things.

An Explorer works best when paired with a detail-sensitive person who understands his great vision – and can set a practical course for getting there. Juan Sebastian del Cano was Magellan's second-in-command. I'd like to give this Spaniard some of the credit for the circumnavigation of the world (and actually making it home alive).

How do you spot Explorers? Boundless energy is their most obvious trait. Explorers are always coming up with new ideas or rushing headlong into new adventures. Do you know what the three *Fortune* 500 companies Auto-Nation, BLOCKBUSTER, and Waste Management have in common? They all owe their existence to a great modern-day Explorer named Wayne Huizenga.

With a single trash truck, Huizenga launched the enterprise that would become Waste Management in 1962 and built the business into a *Fortune* 500 company. Next, he set his sights on a fledging video-rental business... and eventually sold BLOCKBUSTER to Viacom in a deal valued at more than $8 billion. Huizenga then turned his attention to the auto industry, introducing a chain of mega-car dealerships whose website, *www.autonation.com*, pioneered online car buying. In between these other projects, he found time to launch Extended Stay America and buy a few professional sports teams.

Surely this hard-working Explorer's goal was never to be a trash-hauling king, emperor of video rentals, or the czar of cars. Such business leaders set out to build something from nothing, to infuse a company with their visions of "the possible." Huizenga is the epitome of the boundlessly energetic Explorer.

Not every Explorer operates on such a global scale. All around us, Explorers are developing new ideas (perhaps even new ways of running *your* business) without being asked. If an employee brainstorms a great idea at 4:45 that needs an hour of someone else's analysis before a fax can be sent, he's an Explorer.

Explorers don't watch clocks, count the days until the weekend, or dread Mondays. If an Explorer seems to be lost in daydreams during a staff meeting, odds are he's just mentally playing with the universe. Like Wayne Huizenga, Explorers are always looking out for the next million-dollar idea.

You won't usually find Explorers working on the assembly line or driving delivery trucks (a garbage truck perhaps...). Their lack of interest in details means they're not often in accounting. You'll more likely find them in the entrepreneurial ranks, in sales, marketing, or advertising. Research and development has its fair share of Explorers – but only those R&D departments with particularly dynamic environments.

Explorers have often worked a variety of jobs. Yet their checkered job histories will be more than just a string of lifeguard, bartender, and poolboy positions. An Explorer may bounce from sales to high tech to advertising to restaurant management. Their work is their life, so it must be interesting. When they brag, they tell you what they've done, not what they've earned. Money is a by-product of their work, not the reason for it.

> **Their contagious enthusiasm may even inspire the rest of your crew to seek new shores of success.**

Explorers can be excellent salespeople, creative geniuses, and charismatic leaders. Their often contagious enthusiasm may even inspire the rest of your crew to seek out new shores of success. But Explorers need handlers to swab up behind them. All their energy and insight comes at a cost.

Employees who just want to put in an eight-hour day often see the Explorer's constant motion as a threat to workplace predictability. And they aren't the only ones to clash with the Explorer's adventurous spirit. Explorers drive methodical people nuts. Methodical workers proceed in a neat, linear fashion from A to B to C to D. They categorize each task in a project, prioritize its components, and then handle each component in its turn.

Explorers go from A to M to seven to green to Wednesday to – ? It is the seeming randomness of their brains that leads to their insights.[†] An Explorer would put catsup on ice cream just to try it. To methodical people, Explorers are just plain crazy.

I once knew an Explorer in the enviable position of owning a business poised to profit in its first year. After nine difficult start-up months, Mary had her little ship of commerce on an even keel, with a customer base for her direct-mail health products growing exponentially. Deciding it was time to recreate her company's graphic identity, Mary approached me for a complete overhaul of her catalog, a new color scheme for the company... even a brand-new logo! I found her inclination to rock the boat at this stage a little odd, until I realized she was just bored.

Resisting Mary's impulse to send me more business, I tried to help her identify her true needs. Familiar with her retail background, I offered a hypothetical situation: "You run a start-up retail outfit and break even in the first year. Just then, you receive a welcome opportunity to expand your store's size to accommodate its growing sales. With a loyal, growing customer base and the business poised for increased profits, do you think this would be the best time to start tinkering with the store's identity and brand appearance?" "Of course not!" she replied.

Her new venture was a success – and therein lay her problem. It was the chaos and unpredictability of the launch that thrilled Mary most. I suggested she hire a manager and buy herself a motorcycle. She hired several managers,

---

[†] I say "*seeming* randomness," because sometimes these people have minds that truly work in a random (i.e., chaotic) fashion, and other times they're just so darn smart that the rest of us simply can't keep up with them.

then bought that motorcycle... and a sports car. Two years later, Mary sold her business at a handsome profit and was busy developing two more ideas. She's having a ball.

The "life is good" attitude is a common Explorer trait. Take my friend Peter, a true entrepreneur, a dreamer with wild and wonderful ideas. I was wishing him good luck on his latest venture recently, and he told me, "It *has* to work! I've already burned my boat on the beach and am heading inland!" Like all Explorers, the only direction he sees is forward, yesterday's setback is just today's challenge, and to give up is to die!

> The competition will change, as will the marketplace. "Adapt or die" is as true in business as in nature.

With such an attitude, Explorers often scare their bosses, as well as their colleagues. Explorers represent change, and we usually can't help seeing only the risk change portends rather than the possibilities. Yet, as Mary knew, change brings vitality to our work (and our lives). In fact, without it, our businesses are doomed. The competition will change, as will the marketplace itself. "Adapt or die" is as true in the business world as in nature.

What comes to mind when you hear the word *Diebold*? The locks on your front door, the ATM at the corner? Within a dozen years of founding the Diebold Safe & Lock Co. in 1859, German immigrant Charles Diebold held patents on more than 65 different safes. In 1875, his company built the world's largest bank vault for Wells Fargo.

By the first half of the 20th century, Diebold inventors and engineers were busy with time-delay locks, modernized vault doors, even a tear-gas system to deter John

Dillinger-era bank robbers. In 1967, Diebold demonstrated its prototype of the first multi-function ATM at a bankers' conference. Today, Diebold is a world leader in electronic security systems large and small. The company's motto – *We won't rest.* – couldn't be more apt.

Business owners and managers tend to focus only on the products they create or services they provide. It is the rare person who focuses on what the customer actually wants. The Explorer has this gift. Diebold must be especially blessed with Explorers to have had a nearly 150-year history of repeatedly reinventing itself. The leaders at Diebold have maintained their focus on the customers' real need – the safekeeping of valuables – regardless of whether that protection took the form of a walk-in bank vault or a stand-alone ATM.

To manage an Explorer well, you must be both open to his ideas and capable of resisting their allure.

If you're fortunate enough to have any Explorers on your crew, your greatest management challenge is channeling their creative energy. Take some time with them. Ask them what they would do differently if they were in charge. Ask what tools they need to succeed both in your business and in their careers.

And then, act on what you've heard. Paying lip service to an Explorer's needs is worse than not asking him questions at all. Without your support, the Explorer will soon seek opportunities elsewhere.

When the King of Portugal showed no interest in his dream of finding a new route to the East Indies, Magellan turned to neighboring Spain – and made history for the

Spanish crown. Remember this when you have the opportunity to support an Explorer. You don't want to end up like Portugal, when you could be Spain and control most of the New World.

To manage an Explorer well, you must be both open to his ideas and capable of resisting their allure. This isn't as easy as it sounds! We naturally resist suggestions that are not our own, especially when we feel those suggestions would change the very nature of our business.

So, just keep in mind that the Explorer is always looking at what your business can *be*, not what it already is. (Isn't that why you brought him on board, after all?) Invite him to explain the thought process behind his ideas. The more unusual or ambitious the idea, the more details needed.

When Frederick Banting and Charles Best isolated insulin from a pancreas and began injecting it into diabetic dogs in the early 1920s, they had to do a lot of convincing before anyone would allow them to try such an experiment on a human being. Today, their crazy idea is responsible for turning what was once a death sentence – a diabetes diagnosis – into a treatable condition.

If the potential benefits are great but so is the risk, let the Explorer know that's the reason for your decision to say no. If the timing isn't good, ask the Explorer to keep the idea on a back burner. And if this week's idea is just a little too far-fetched for you, emphasize how you appreciate the Explorer's creativity. For an Explorer, life is an endless brainstorming session. And like any good brainstorming session, every so often one of those crazy ideas tossed on the table turns out to be a real gem.

As the manager, however, take care not to get as carried away with the Explorer's big ideas as he does. While the Explorer fixes his eye on the horizon, you must watch out for small shoals along the way known as cash-flow problems, personnel issues, sales reports, and so on. You certainly don't want to constrain an Explorer with too many rules or too much structure. (If your Explorer shows up at 10:00 a.m., did he have a breakfast meeting with a potentially lucrative new client?) But you must provide clearly defined responsibilities, expectations, and budgets.

These guidelines are all the more important because of how the rest of the crew sees the Explorer. All too often

Explorers' Talents

- They are creative, visionary, constantly thinking about opportunities, and can have breakthrough ideas.
- They are ambitious, enthusiastic, and excited about life.
- They work hard and are willing volunteers.
- They have a range of experiences.
- They are confident and comfortable with themselves.
- They move quickly towards their goals.
- They are interesting to others.
- They manage their time well (although their schedules may appear chaotic or random to the rest of the crew).

Explorers' Drawbacks

- They don't understand the need to spend time on employee harmony.
- They can have volatile temperaments.
- They can become bored with the details of a plan.
- They usually require highly organized assistants.
- They can drive very organized people crazy.
- They would rather work independently.
- They require flexible schedules.

they focus on the "special treatment" an Explorer supposedly enjoys. They do not recognize, or won't acknowledge, the Explorer's correspondingly higher responsibilities.

The magazine world offers a good example of this tendency. Long hours, frequent travel to industry shows and other events in unappealing destinations, a persistent perception of being underpaid... A magazine writer tells me such job-related trials cause many editors to look longingly at their advertising counterparts. Newcomers often grumble or express surprise that the salespeople have things "so easy": flexible hours, credit cards, a car allowance. Never having placed a cold call to a potential advertiser, they don't realize the challenges of closing the deal, ad page after ad page, month after month – and that the better you do, the higher the bar is set.

> **In exchange for a little flexibility and perks, you should expect your Explorers to perform twice as well.**

In exchange for a little flexibility and perks, Explorers should be expected to perform twice as well as the average employee – whether productivity is defined by sales figures, hours billed, production costs reduced, grants received, or new inventions developed. By sharing those expectations with the entire crew, you'll eliminate some of the misconceptions about special treatment. You'll also open the door to advancement for others. With your guidelines in writing, however, most pretenders to the title of Explorer will hesitate and "let you know" about their seriousness for advancement. And almost every one of them will later say, "Thanks, but no thanks."

This is probably a good thing, for, like spices in the ship's galley, a little Explorer can go a long way. Remember, there was only one Magellan for an entire five-ship fleet! Your Explorers will inspire you to sail for new lands, but you must also consider who will chart the course, trim the sails, and heave the anchor when you reach shore.

What If You Are an Explorer?

First, take a long look in the mirror. Which activities do you truly enjoy? Which projects or tasks would you be happy never doing again? Explorers have wonderful gifts, but they don't do everything well. If you have the blood of an Explorer in you, determine whether you are stifling that side of your personality by busying yourself with things you really don't like (and perhaps aren't even good at doing).

Once you acknowledge your strengths and passions, take steps to restructure your business life. Administrative burdens? Computer headaches? Personnel problems? Get help. Accounting, sales, marketing, production, shipping, human resources, even answering the phone... Get help! Free your time to do the things you're passionate about and at which you excel. Just make sure the economic value you create by being an Explorer will pay for all the assistance you require.

Yet sometimes an Explorer needs more than just additional Crew Members to be happy. Sometimes an Explorer is ready for a whole new ship. Consider: If you won the lottery, would you keep doing what you do today? If so, you have your dream job. If not, what would you do? Life is too short and unpredictable to wait for the lottery. Old fears about setting a new course may not even have any basis in reality anymore. Start moving toward that vision of what your work and your life can be. And, as you set out, think of Wayne Huizenga, who began with one trash truck and now owns the Miami Dolphins.

CHAPTER THREE

The Navigator

A good Navigator can be an Explorer's best friend. Once an Explorer identifies his destination, he needs someone capable of setting the course to that far-off land, and of overseeing the ship's progress once under way. A Navigator knows the water depth and wind patterns, dangerous reefs and prevailing currents. If an Explorer wishes to cross the Atlantic Ocean from Europe to the Americas, his Navigator can recommend a Northern, mid-Atlantic, or Southern route, and then chart a general course for reaching that distant shore.

Just as important a gift as his knowledge of the sea is the Navigator's flexibility. Familiar with the sea's different stormy seasons, the Navigator knows firsthand how necessary course corrections are to ensure a successful voyage. Explorers are sometimes so wedded to their dreams that, left to themselves, they will not deviate from the initial course plan for achieving them. Flexible but still focused on the goal – reaching those shores – the Navigator does not get locked into the details of a journey too soon in the planning process.

The tireless Commodore George Anson of the *Centurion* embodies the Navigator's flexibility. Setting sail from England in 1740, the ship encountered violent storms that resulted in a total loss of the crew's bearings. When he finally dropped anchor at what they thought was Juan Fernandez Island in the South Pacific, Anson discovered they were at the Western tip of Tierra del Fuego instead. After zigzagging East and West for another few months, Anson finally brought his ship and crew into safe port.

Unlike the Explorer, a Navigator will not boldly go where no man has gone before. The Segway Human Transporter wasn't the brainchild of a Navigator! But you can bet that scores of Navigators at other companies are working out how to get in on such futuristic forms of transportation. A Navigator's talents lie in the identification and analysis of prevailing and emerging trends. You can rely on him to spot new opportunities for success and then adjust a business plan or corporate strategy to pursue those opportunities.

Explorers can be possessive about their ideas; Navigators just want to use the idea to reach the goal.

The genesis of the company that would one day be known as the Golden Arches illustrates what can happen when smart Explorers team up with a savvy Navigator. Brothers Dick and Mac McDonald opened a hamburger stand in San Bernardino, California, in 1948. Their formula was unheard of in the restaurant industry: a limited menu, low prices, fast service, no frills, and a Multimixer whipping up to five milkshakes at a time.

The McDonalds were indeed pioneers, and very successful ones at that. So successful, in fact, that by the mid-1950s they had duplicated their little hamburger joint in eight other locations around California and Arizona – and were profiting 100 grand a year!

Enter a middle-aged Multimixer salesman named Ray Kroc, so curious about the McDonald brothers' extraordinary success that he drove from Chicago to California to take a peek at their operation. What Kroc saw amazed him: a nine-item menu, customers standing in line at all hours of the day, 15-cent burgers selling as fast as they came off the grill, and Multimixers running non-stop!

A true Navigator, Kroc just had to get involved. Perhaps thinking he could make his fortune off the potential Multimixer sales, Kroc suggested the brothers open up a few more restaurants. When the McDonalds asked him who'd launch any more new locations, Kroc replied, "What about me?" The rest is business history. Kroc's success building the McDonald's empire was due to more than just his ability to spot a new opportunity in the restaurant industry's trend towards "faster" food. Kroc was able to shift his own course plan for making money from selling Multimixers to selling hamburgers.

It's great to be an Explorer, your mind brimming with unique ideas. But, sometimes it's even better to be the Navigator and fulfill the dream. Ray Kroc and Juan Sebastian del Cano actually completed their journeys.

It's not always smooth sailing, however. The relationship between the Explorer and the Navigator is often a stormy one. Explorers can be possessive about their ideas; Navigators just want to use the idea to reach the goal, and may even consider the Explorer an obstacle to that success.

Conflicts are inevitable when market conditions require a change in plans, yet the Explorer is adamant about maintaining the original course.

Problems of conflict aside, it's good to have a Navigator on board. Once he embraces a business's goals, the Navigator will ably guide that business towards success. A Navigator is not swayed by dreams of making a big statement, getting his 15 minutes of fame, or seeing his name in spotlights. He doesn't care if he's the first to sail around the world; he wants to discover a *better* way to reach the Spice Islands and make his fortune. Not the breakthrough inventor type, the Navigator is the one who'll take the invention and make it better. He's okay holding second place at the start of the race: When the leader tires, he knows he'll pull ahead and win the race.

Take Henry Ford, the man whose name is eternally linked to the automobile. Of course, Ford's great invention was not the automobile: It was the assembly line. This manufacturing innovation enabled him to produce cars more cheaply than anyone else, thereby turning a luxury product into a necessity of modern life.

Ford's "cheap" cars changed the face of the world: Luxury automobiles from dozens of different high-end manufacturers wound through the streets of American cities in the 1920s and 1930s. Where are they now? Gone, their names familiar to few but collectors. But who hasn't heard of Henry Ford?! His assembly line has influenced every manufacturing business around the globe.

Navigators can imagine their world six months, 12 months, even 24 months ahead. What a typical Navigator does not make a habit of is trying to imagine things 20 *years* ahead. On board a freighter, you wouldn't find the Navigator wasting time plotting voyages years in advance, would you? Weather, cargo weight, port schedules... He must contend with too many variables. And, besides, his ship has scores of trips to complete successfully between now and then.

In the business world, too, Navigators live in the here and now – gathering information and reacting to stimuli around them, then drawing on knowledge and experience to move towards a goal one step at a time. Let's take an example from the biotech industry: a research team charged with developing a stand-alone machine that conducts real-time detection of cancerous cells from a single droplet of blood. This team's Navigator doesn't spend his working hours imagining the day when handheld *Star Trek*-type medical scanners conduct complete physicals with a swipe of the arm.

> **On board a freighter, you wouldn't find the Navigator wasting time plotting voyages years in advance.**

Yes, that may be the future towards which he and his colleagues are working. But today's challenge is how to detect the disease cells in a lab setting, then how to develop a prototype machine, then how to make the prototype commercially viable, and so on, and so on.

These methodical individuals are usually born, not made. They aren't clock-watchers and won't usually be found on the assembly line or doing clerical work. Chefs, salespeople, scientists, teachers... You're more likely to find Navigators among such groups. Navigators tend not to be union members, because they don't see themselves as mere cogs in a large wheel, toiling for a weekly paycheck. Confident and often creative, some Navigators have worked a wide variety of jobs in their chosen field, or even switched careers – past experiences from which they draw ideas for solving today's challenges.

Stepping up to any challenge with a realistic plan of action is the Navigator's most obvious characteristic. I recall a particularly frustrating staff meeting to discuss a few "issues" we were experiencing with a client. I tossed the problem on the table and waited for one of my five employees present to respond. Silence. Four pairs of eyes looked back at me, their messages pretty clear: "This is not my problem," "Leave me alone," "I'm going home in three hours," perhaps even, "I really can't forget to buy cat food after work."

> **Confident and often creative, some Navigators have worked a wide variety of jobs in their chosen field.**

The fifth person then said, "I've noticed that every time we propose this type of solution, the client doesn't like it. But when we change it in *this* way, the client is happy. I propose that we follow this alternative path from now on." Ahhh – a Navigator to the rescue! Here was someone willing to step from behind the protective wall of his job description and make a few course corrections on the path to success with this valuable client.

Like Explorers, Navigators know that the business world is as dynamic as the weather at sea. Course corrections are a part of life – even within the environment of a small business. This flexibility is as important a skill as the Navigator's ability to set a course when handed a goal. Henry Ford eventually halted production of his beloved Model T, because the rest of the industry was starting to copy his production techniques to lower their own costs. *Voilà!* Ford introduced the Model A design.

A classic Navigator, Ford understood that change is good – as long as it's not just change for the sake of change, but part of a real and necessary evolution of the business.

Navigators tend to announce themselves, so they're not difficult to spot. After you've worked with a Navigator awhile, he may ask if you have time to review a few new

Navigators' Talents
- They are organized and flexible.
- They are intelligent.
- They are dependable and hard-working.
- They are ambitious and confident.
- They have a range of experiences.
- They encourage harmony at work.
- They are excited about new opportunities.
- They are good at developing the details of a plan.
- They enjoy the puzzle of determining how to meet a new challenge.
- They can help bring good ideas to fruition.
- They move steadily towards their goals.
- They are aware of others' styles.
- They can have consistent temperaments.
- They know how to delegate.
- They manage their time well.

Navigators' Drawbacks
- They don't usually have breakthrough ideas of their own.
- They can become bored with too much routine.
- They will sometimes get involved in projects where they have no expertise.

ideas. He's likely to share thoughts with you about projects or tasks outside his normal responsibilities. Navigators need room to run, but it's best if it occurs within a defined space. A Navigator's imagination is not as bold or wild as an Explorer's, but it's usually more productive.

When bringing a Navigator on board, do more than just get him up to speed on your company's goals and ideas for the future. Share the history of your business with him. To do what they do best – map a course for the future – Navigators must know how your company got where it is. They should understand industry trends and background stories on your competitors. Unlike an Explorer, whose face is always set towards the future, a Navigator will embrace the lessons of the past.

Navigators can be highly linear thinkers, so they want to get things right before they take action. It's a good sign, not a waste of time, if a Navigator returns with more questions. The more information Navigators have, the better their decisions will be. So, when a Navigator proposes changes, listen carefully. He's probably given the ideas a good deal of thought.

A few years ago, an Explorer who was micromanaging his apparel business to death approached me to design marketing materials. This man involved himself in the work of his 300 employees to the point of their exasperation. He clearly thought he was the only person who could do things the right way. (Sound familiar?) He would announce sweeping new rules and then break them himself. The last retort was always, "I own this company." Skilled workers soon left, and poor ones stayed forever. The quality of his crew sunk lower and lower.

Finally, a failed marriage seemed to be the catalyst for this Explorer to make changes at work: He turned active management of the company over to the first of what would become a series of Navigators. Each Navigator came on board ambitious and eager to correct the company's downward spiral. The Explorer listened for a while – then fired each of them in turn.

Eventually this Explorer hired a Navigator who was particularly skilled in the tactful art of presenting solutions that the Explorer thought were his own ideas. That latest Navigator is still on the job, the quality of the crew has skyrocketed, and the company's outlook is positive at last.

If you have a Navigator on your crew, you are blessed with a flexible and capable talent. Thank your lucky stars you have someone on board who can chart the way to new and potentially more profitable shores – and who will take in stride those unexpected stormy seas your ship encounters on the way.

What If **You** Are a Navigator?

Keep a lookout for Explorers! As a business owner or manager with the talents listed above, you should have no difficulty keeping an eye on the competition by yourself. Maintaining a steady course is no problem for a Navigator. Yet to envision what your business can become – what unimagined seas are waiting to be sailed – you probably need an Explorer's insight. So when you spot an Explorer, pick his brains. You may need his ideas for new products or services to bring to market.

Finding an Explorer takes a little sleuthing outside of the workplace. You're not necessarily looking for a new business partner or employee, after all. Your interaction with Explorers can be as formal as a mentoring relationship or as casual as a conversation with the guy in the airplane seat next to you. What you're looking for is someone to help you picture your world 20 years, not 20 months, from now.

Explorers are scattered all around us: a neighbor, your kid's soccer coach, a member of a client's firm, perhaps a schoolteacher who's also an amateur chemist… or an aficionado of European coffee. (Think of Howard Schultz, who in 1982 began his transformation of a small coffee shop across from the Seattle fish market into an international phenomenon called Starbucks, coming soon to a Target store near you.) Just keep looking!

As for your crew, your first duty as Navigator is to communicate the ship's course to everyone on board. Then, ask your crew members what individual contributions they can make towards a profitable voyage. Once the details are in place, delegate – always taking time to recognize your subordinates' successes.

When it is necessary to alter course as you refine your business and tackle new markets, remember that change scares many people. Explain your changes in advance, <u>and</u> the benefits both ship and crew will receive from them. Your crew will then be prepared to weather any unexpected squalls while feeling as safe and comfortable as possible.

CHAPTER FOUR

The Captain

Hundreds of courageous men managed the Spanish *galeónes* that criss-crossed the seas from the 15th to the 17th centuries between the Old World and the New. These Captains didn't have to ponder whether their trips were worth making, or try to figure out new markets for the cacao beans and tobacco filling their holds. Their course of action was spelled out in quite simple terms: "Sail west with supplies, sail east with gold. Sail west with supplies, sail east with gold. Avoid storms and watch for pirates. Repeat as often as possible."

Gold and silver, the primary objectives of the conquistadors, flowed into Spain with unmatched splendor. These riches fueled the amazing economic engine of the Spanish Empire, which resulted in a brilliant cultural, artistic, and intellectual life. The Spaniards owe much of this to their Captains in the Age of Exploration.

Skilled in sailing and navigation, in managing precious cargo and cantankerous crews, these Captains did their jobs and did them well. They did not design and construct the ships, devise the "sail-east, sail-west" business plan, or locate markets for newly discovered wares. Others had done those tasks before them. The Captains' job was to get those ships back and forth, safely and swiftly.

In business, a ship's Captain is the ultimate steward of capitalism. He understands *why* a business exists and will not stray from either the Explorer's vision or the Navigator's plan. Under his able command, a good Captain can direct any ship of commerce to profitability and success.

Most evident among the Captain's talents, in fact, is that he tends to be a jack-of-all-trades. He knows the fundamentals of sales, accounting, engineering, human resources, legal, manufacturing, research and development, or anything else he might run across. He can switch roles as needed to address his business's most immediate projects or challenges. He sees beyond the unique products or services his company provides: He knows it's not about shoes or hamburgers – but about all the steps in the chain that make a business complete.

> **You might even say a good Captain is the ideal parent: He doesn't play favorites and knows when to let go.**

Yet a good Captain doesn't micromanage. He possesses sufficient people skills to hire and retain a talented crew. (And he knows the wisdom of hiring people smarter than he is.) Confident in his Crew Members' abilities, the Captain knows he can trust their decisions, and so leaves them to work in peace. You might even say a good Captain is the ideal parent: He doesn't play favorites, is never too busy to offer encouragement or advice, remains watchful for opportunities to excel and disasters to avoid, and knows when to let go.

THE CAPTAIN

Jack Welch is the epitome of the good Captain. Named CEO of General Electric Co. in 1981 at age 44, he took over the helm of a company with $25 billion in annual sales and more than 400,000 employees. As a good Captain should, Welch sought ways to streamline operations and improve productivity. Enhanced training and mentoring allowed Welch to trim the ranks, as fewer workers were required to accomplish the same tasks.

He focused the company's efforts on what it did well, and dropped what it did not (tough decisions that soon earned Welch the nickname "Neutron Jack"). And he developed his aptly named "vitality curve." The curve divided General Electric's employees into three groups: the top 20 percent were rewarded handsomely; the middle 70 percent received modest raises; and the bottom 10 percent received nothing extra.

The significance of Welch's vitality curve was that the top group did not consist of just senior executives. The top group comprised the company's best workers, whether they toiled in a corner office at headquarters or the mailroom at a satellite plant.[†] GE gradually earned a reputation as a great place to work – *if* you were a great worker – and became the model of a well-run business.

Of course, not all Captains can be described as "good," as our media headlines offer frequent proof: Enron, WorldCom, KPMG, AIG, Tyco. Even more insidious than the truly awful Captains, however, are the merely mediocre.

[†]According to Welch's 2001 book *Jack: Straight from the Gut*, top-20 employees displayed traits ranging from a passion for their work and an openness to ideas from every quarter, to such leadership qualities as the ability to rally others around a common goal.

Untimely and well-deserved ends often await disastrous Captains. Unfortunately, mediocre Captains can hang in there for entire careers.

Years ago, I had the "opportunity" to work with one of these mediocre Captains. Bob's particular ship was a department within a larger company for which my firm was designing a new magazine template. As we worked on the project, Bob would drop off proofs or other materials

Captains' Talents

- They have well-rounded backgrounds and experience in management.
- They are familiar with all the systems of their business.
- They can work hard.
- They are ambitious.
- They are trustworthy.
- They are often intelligent.
- They can shift responsibilities quickly.
- They are happy when things go well.
- They take pride in their work.
- They can implement the details of a plan and oversee the fulfillment of ideas.
- They can have consistent temperaments.
- They know how to delegate.
- They can prioritize tasks and manage their time well.

Captains' Drawbacks

- They don't usually have breakthrough ideas of their own.
- Their routine can lead to laziness and carelessness.
- They can be "career clock watchers."
- They will avoid projects where they have no expertise.
- They can be inflexible.
- They may stay involved in a business where they no longer add any value.

for my crew on his way into the office (around 9:30 a.m.) or on his way home (around 3:30 p.m.). My employees soon realized the man's workday was just six hours long – even if he worked through lunch!

His cushy hours weren't the only thing to amaze them. His department's major responsibility was the design and production of a full-color magazine. Bob delegated this important task to a junior employee, while he handled just a simple newsletter. Bob's subordinate frequently complained to me about this awkward situation in which he found himself. Why would a department's most skilled and senior person take on the simplest task and leave a junior in charge of the most critical work? Hmm… What do you think was going on here? Bob was just waiting for his gold watch. Too bad he still had 20 years to go.

> **Inappropriate delegating, whether to a subordinate or a committee, is the weak Captain's little trick.**

The average Captain – who often knows he's average and is terrified of making a mistake – is easily spotted by such inactivity. When faced with a challenge, the mediocre Captain first tries to defer responsibility to a subordinate. If the subordinate is skilled and takes effective action, problem solved. If not, the Captain lets the subordinate take the fall.

If the Captain has no subordinate ready at hand, he may convene a committee to study the problem (and, perhaps, a committee to study the work of that committee, followed by another committee to summarize the findings of the first two…). Inappropriate delegating, whether to a subordinate or a committee, is the weak Captain's little trick to avoid making a decision that might be the wrong one. A good Captain doesn't worry about taking responsibility: He's secure in the knowledge that past experiences have given him the insight to evaluate any challenge and formulate a viable solution.

Even Captains with solid careers behind them may succumb to the critical weakness of inactivity. This usually strikes five or 10 years before their projected retirement dates. The Captain feels his age prevents him from switching careers or moving to another company, and so... he does nothing. Avoiding risk is key. The goal is simply to hang on, as some invisible clock moves ever so slowly towards his last day of work. It's as if, after years at the helm, the Captain suddenly loses his sea legs and must cling to the mast or tumble overboard.

Passing time becomes the name of the game, so watch out for Captains suddenly fond of two-hour lunches. If the company is sufficiently large or prosperous, such Captains are tolerated by an unwritten code of senior management:

It's as if, after years at the helm, the Captain suddenly loses his sea legs and must cling to the mast.

If you've put in a reasonable amount of time and were a good Captain, we'll just let you drift towards the shores of retirement. What a waste! Good Captains possess a lifetime of valuable experience they could share with the next generation. Far better for these retiring leaders to mentor the future Captains already moving up the ranks behind them.

Captains come from two different backgrounds. Some start from the ground up, rising through the ranks from Crew Member to First Mate, perhaps serving a stint as Navigator. We've all heard the stories of the guy who "started in the mailroom" and ended in the boardroom managing tens of thousands of employees.

Less dramatic but equally impressive examples abound. Some years back, I heard about the head of a powerhouse advertising and PR firm with four offices and more than 100 employees. It seemed all the leading politicians, banks, and corporations in our area had either worked with her firm or thought about it. What was this incredible woman's background? She had started out as a receptionist at another large ad agency in town.

The second background typical of a Captain is the path of professional education and training. After receiving their degrees, these future leaders move on to junior management positions in sales or product development, finance or accounting. Job switches come along with new and better titles, until their leadership qualities win them the coveted Captain's position.

Each path to the position of Captain has its benefits. The school of hard knocks boasts a tough curriculum, but its lessons really sink in, providing the self-taught Captain great common-sense solutions for future challenges. The more formally educated Captain, on the other hand, enters the work world armed with extensive historical perspective. The downside can be a lack of street smarts, but in a few years a well-schooled Captain will catch up with his self-taught counterpart.

Self-taught Captains, however, must continue to be just that: self-taught. It's not for nothing that students still read Machiavelli's *The Prince*! The pages of history teach much about leadership, power, and the rules of competition –

but you must open the book. And, regardless of his background, a good Captain understands the need to keep abreast of developments in technology and other subjects required to steer his particular ship.

A company run by a combination of Explorers and Navigators will usually lurch forward with some success if the business concept itself is solid. With a good Captain at the helm, however, the voyage is sure to be a much more pleasant one. Rough seas feel a little less uncomfortable when a steady hand is on the tiller. Loyal and able to subordinate his personal needs to those of the business, a good Captain makes life on board much more enjoyable for everyone.

After you've determined that your Captain is indeed a good one, management issues are fairly straightforward. The Explorer envisions that distant shore, and the Navigator charts a course to get there – but it is the Captain who actually cries, "Hoist the sails!" and gets you under way. So make sure he knows where you're headed!

A good Captain will perform admirably, if given clear expectations. If yours is a large company, you may have a Captain heading each department. A smaller enterprise might require just one Captain to take the day-to-day job of running the ship off the owner's hands.

In either case, responsibilities must be spelled out in writing. Your Captain should know your business plan, strategies, and goals as well as a sailor knows the tides. He must also understand the terms of his performance evaluations, including whether his success will be measured by the company's financial health.

THE CAPTAIN

Once under way, maintain contact with your Captain to ensure the voyage is going smoothly. This may sound obvious, but communication breakdowns plague many smaller businesses: The owner sets up shop, installs the Captain and crew, and disappears.

I recently heard about an entrepreneur who opened three businesses in a row (two in the hospitality industry and one a service provider) and is now preparing to buy a fourth. She barely gets one up and running before she starts negotiating purchase of another. The businesses have managed to limp along so far without a solid management team in place; but employee turnover is high and morale couldn't be lower. Her little ships of commerce are floating around without a Captain in sight, and the owner isn't even watching them from the dock.

> **Your Captain should know your business plan, strategies, and goals as well as a sailor knows the tides.**

Larger organizations don't work this way – so why do many independent business owners think it will work on a small scale? Most of the world's mid-sized and large businesses consist of multiple divisions with varying degrees of autonomy. Department heads handle the daily decisions and operations, reporting to their superiors on a regular basis. The supervisors' broader perspective allows them to give individual division heads clarification about changes in goals or strategies.

No well-run corporation would allow individual divisions to run *completely* by the local leaders' own rules. After all, each division is still a part of the larger organization and exists to contribute to that organization's financial health. The single ship is still part of a larger fleet.

A good Captain should be an excellent caretaker for your business. Major changes in the marketplace, overhauls of your product lineup, or an unexpected move by the competition may unsteady him for the moment. With your Navigator at the ready to plot any needed course corrections, however, the Captain will keep that ship headed towards the safety of land.

What If <u>You</u> Are a Captain?

Compare your own management of crew and cargo with that of "Neutron Jack." Do you reward your highest-valued people – the top producers, the most-skilled Crew Members, the employees at the heart of your business? Or, do you pass out raises and promotions based on mere seniority? Poor performers can drag your business under by alienating customers and sowing disaffection among the rest of the crew. Do you have the guts to toss malcontents and Stowaways overboard when necessary to ensure the safety of the entire ship?

Managing your cargo is almost as important as managing the crew. Take a look below decks: Are you saving outdated products just because you have a warehouse full of them? Or do you regularly work with your Explorer and Navigator to develop new products or services that customers actually want to buy? As Captain, it's not your job to set the goals and chart the course. But that doesn't mean you should blindly steer into troubled waters just because "we've always done it this way." A business will stay afloat only as long as people need what you sell. So, talk to your customers and keep an eye on the horizon.

CHAPTER FIVE

The First Mate

Let's heave to for a few minutes and review the shipboard characters we've met so far. We have the Explorer, the dreamer with the breakthrough ideas. We have a Navigator, the detail person, skilled in charting routes that turn vision into reality. And we have our Captain, the leader who oversees the ship's crew and systems to keep the vessel on course and out of harm's way.

You could say these three individuals operate beyond a ship's physical boundaries: As they work, they are always conscious of their cargo, the final port, the markets in that city, and numerous attendant details.

Meanwhile, our ship carries a contingent of workers: deck hands, cooks, engineers, radio operators, a maintenance crew, and many others. Such a diverse group of Crew Members requires someone who can communicate the Explorer's, Navigator's, and Captain's needs to them. The First Mate is that person. The First Mate may not actually know *how* to tend the engines or work the radios or cook for a crew of 200, but he knows the people who do.

Aboard ship, the First Mate doesn't necessarily do all the work – he makes sure it gets done.

In business, a First Mate is the soul of the operation. I know that sounds like a bit much: Aren't Explorers, Navigators, and, certainly, Captains more important? But by soul, I mean the pivotal point, to use a more common metaphor – that spot on which the balance of excellence or mediocrity, of success or failure, ultimately rests. A First Mate can make the difference between a business that merely survives and one that truly thrives.

The First Mate doesn't always hold a high-profile job, yet he has the political savvy and inherent "people skills" to grease the skids and work out differences. A business can grow without a First Mate serving as tactful intermediary between the "higher ups" and the "little guys," but without one the daily workflow and overall development may be choppy at best.

> **Quiet efficiency is another mark of the First Mate. One of my favorite First Mates is Radar from M*A*S*H.**

First Mates are comfortable people to have around. Not flashy, they move in like the fog and quietly accomplish things. They are honest and kind, and people like them. First Mates know their own gifts and shortcomings. The gifts, they enhance. The shortcomings, they work on. They are curious and enjoy learning. And, they are always available to help. They may not be noticed by many, but their efforts to keep everything shipshape and on schedule are appreciated by all.

The First Mate's ability to foster cooperation is perhaps his greatest asset in the workplace. Explorers, Navigators, and

THE FIRST MATE

Captains can become so consumed by a goal that they offend the people below them. Subordinates often interpret as "abrupt" or "pompous" the behavior that a Captain would just describe as "being efficient" or "getting the job done." People at the top can alienate a crew and even provoke them to mutiny. A true First Mate steps in to smooth over these little rough passages and keeps the crew working in harmony.

Quiet efficiency is another mark of the First Mate. One of my favorite First Mates is Radar from the television series M*A*S*H. Radar manages to keep Colonel Blake, the Army unit's leader, on track. As if by magic, paperwork appears beneath the Colonel's hand the moment it's needed; and, no matter how loud the party, Radar hears the choppers coming in with wounded before anyone else does. Radar maintains a smooth rhythm to the business of the camp, in spite of the chaos of war and the craziness of fellow characters Hawkeye and Trapper John. Good job, Radar – you're a first-rate First Mate!

Real-life First Mates also recognize what needs to be done even before the ship's Captain does, or before he says anything about it. And, like Radar, they take care of more than just the boss. In my informal poll of colleagues' First Mates while researching this book, I heard the story of a young woman known affectionately to her co-workers as "our gal Trudy."

Officially, Trudy worked as secretary to the woman in charge of a six-member team of business analysts at a major West Coast insurance carrier. These analysts spent about two-thirds of their time traveling; so, in addition to her administrative duties for the boss, Trudy was expected to handle their basic travel arrangements. This First Mate soon learned, however, that life would be better for everyone (her boss the Captain, the crew, *herself*) if she took on just a few more responsibilities....

Say you were one of the business analysts, and you were scheduled to fly out Sunday evening to spend the next week at an office in Des Moines. Friday afternoon, Trudy would hand over your documents from the travel agency (these were pre-Internet days).

She'd also tell you what size conference room she'd had her counterpart at the Des Moines office reserve for your end-of-week presentation... and that she'd arranged for the slide projector to be set up a day ahead so you could do a practice run. If the corporate culture at the Des Moines office included drinks after work once a week, she'd make sure you knew that little insider tidbit as well.

But Trudy didn't stop there! She would tell you the dress code at the office you'd be visiting... check the local weather forecast for the week ("Don't forget an umbrella!")... and, once you'd left, scout your office to make sure you hadn't left a credit card or important document behind (again). One of the guys on the team liked to watch sports after the business day was over. Trudy was on top of that, too: "The hotel you're at doesn't have a bar, but there's a restaurant with a lounge across the street, and they're open until 11:00."

On the rare occasion she knew the entire team would be in the home office, Trudy scheduled a lunch to celebrate the birthdays that month (even if one was hers). There's nothing, the crew used to say, "our gal Trudy" can't do.

THE FIRST MATE

How did Trudy know enough to make these decisions on her own? She voluntarily sat in on the regular staff meetings – having told the Captain it was much easier for her to do her job if she didn't hear about everyone's upcoming plans and projects second- or third-hand.

With a good Captain and a First Mate like Trudy, you've got an unbeatable team. When it comes to mediocrity at the helm, a First Mate may actually keep the ship on an even keel *despite* a poor Captain. A colleague tells me of just such a First Mate, a senior analyst named Carl with whom she worked back in the days when IT was known as "data processing."

> **Because he was never quite sure what his crew was busy doing, he'd react by making himself look busy.**

Carl's project team – just one of many small ships within the fleet of an enormous corporation – included half a dozen other analysts and programmers. The project manager – the Captain of their tiny vessel – was as benignly inept as they come. Unreasonable requests were his *modus operandi*: If a major deadline loomed at day's end, the Captain was sure to announce a staff meeting for 11:00 that very morning.

The Captain wasn't a mean person, but, because he was never quite sure what his crew was so busy doing, he'd react by making himself look busy. And how does a poor manager look busy? By holding a meeting.

With equal amounts of tact and firmness, Carl would approach the Captain and say something along the lines of: "Staff meeting sounds good – but if we have it this *morning*, we won't get our report in for the $10-million conversion project due at five. It would *really* help us meet today's deadline if you could get those final numbers from accounting for us. They've been giving me the runaround." Did Carl truly need the Captain's help? Of course not! He was getting the man out of the way with busy work so the crew could make their deadline.

The disharmony this Captain's unreasonable edicts caused among the crew never reached his ears: Carl absorbed it like a sponge. His listening skills were as good as his ability to run interference; so, it was in his office, not in the break room, that the crew would scream, "How can he do this?" in frantic frustration. Exuding calm, Carl would wait until the programmer or analyst had himself under control and then focus him back on the work. Thanks to Carl's First Mate skills, that team was as efficient as any other in the division despite their incompetent "leader."

This approach to assembling a crew is like constructing a sailboat with helm, rudders, mast, but no keel.

Even good Captains can be so busy with the details of piloting their ships that they miss the subtleties of morale. First Mates such as Carl are tuned into this. Not out for themselves, these individuals genuinely seek to contribute to the companies they work for and to nurture their fellow shipmates. Their quiet contributions represent a real talent that should not be overlooked.

Unfortunately, too many business owners dismiss the need for a First Mate. Entrepreneurs, developers, managers, a sales team, administrative staff – that's all we need, right? This approach to assembling a crew is like constructing a sailboat with helm, rudder, masts, but no keel.

You've got the means to catch the wind and to maneuver once you've harnessed its power – but without a keel, the entire thing will flop sideways into the water as soon as you leave the dock. You won't be moving anywhere but into a lifeboat.

I was fortunate enough to bring a true gem of a First Mate on board my own ship a few years ago. I hired her for the position of office manager, but she became much more in

First Mates' Talents

- They are dependable and accurate.
- They are honest.
- They have even temperaments.
- They are willing volunteers.
- They will cheerfully do tasks outside their assigned responsibilities.
- They handle challenges and unexpected situations well.
- They are flexible and usually comfortable with change.
- They are self-confident.
- They possess good "people skills."
- They enhance social interaction at work.
- They are efficient with their time.
- They encourage harmony among employees.
- They are loyal.
- They enjoy being part of a team.

First Mates' Drawbacks

- They don't usually have breakthrough ideas.
- They may try to make peace at any price.
- Their creativity may reveal itself only in subtle ways.
- They may hesitate to challenge the boss's poor ideas.
- They may allow others to take advantage of their generous and hard-working natures.
- They may not take the initiative to further their own training or education.

no time. Although her stated responsibilities involve mostly secretarial and bookkeeping duties, she continually looks beyond her job description for opportunities to help. No duty is beneath her. If smudgy handprints mar the glass on the front door, out comes the Windex. She doesn't announce to the world in general, "The door's dirty again! *Someone* should do something about it." She just takes care of it.

Always on an even keel, her mood is unflappable in the worst of situations: our recent sewer line overflow problem, for example. Although it was very unpleasant, she led the charge, found a plumber, supervised the repair, and cleaned up the aftermath. Talk about performance beyond the call of duty!

If she notices a larger problem, one beyond her skill level or authority to resolve, she brings it to my attention – but only after drawing up a recommended solution, a logical course of action, and a budget. If morale is low, she walks in with a baked treat. If a computer is gacking, she seeks out the best in-house expert to handle the problem. Bookkeeping, morale building, janitorial or secretarial... It doesn't matter.

First Mates possess superior "people skills," and mine is no exception. If you're quiet, she'll respect your privacy. Extroverted? She's an eager audience. In turmoil? She offers a safe harbor of comfort. Frantic? She lends soft support until the storm passes. Her courteous demeanor is bulletproof and, perhaps most important in a small office, she does not gossip. Everyone feels safe sharing their stories with her, because we all know they'll never come back to haunt us.

THE FIRST MATE

Looking back, I used to wonder why I hadn't found a good First Mate earlier. I had hired smart people – good, smart people. But, as I eventually realized, I had a tendency to hire good, smart, *young* people. I assumed the enthusiasm of youth would conquer all challenges.

I admit that when I interviewed my current First Mate, I wasn't sure how to deal with a prospective employee who would be older than I am. Not by much, mind you, but older. But she seemed a good fit, so I figured, "What the heck! Let's go for it and see what happens." What happened was the best break I've ever had! She knows her job and, what's more, she *likes* her job and is comfortable with it. Crises don't ruffle her because she's dealt with it all before. She knows there's always a solution. Maturity born of life's experiences is a wonderful gift.

> **If smudgy handprints mar the glass, out comes the Windex. She doesn't announce, "The door's dirty again!"**

Maturity can stem from innate abilities as well as life experience, of course. Both Trudy and Carl were in their early 30s, and many First Mates are much younger than that. When you hear a parent say of their young child, "She's so organized or smart or ambitious, it's like she's 10 going on 30," that kid has the makings of a First Mate.

First Mates have rarely inspired novelists or caught the attention of historians. Yet I'd bet you personally know more First Mates than Explorers, Navigators, and Captains put together.

It's not always easy to spot a First Mate, however, because they don't draw attention to themselves. So if you want to know who's the First Mate at your business, check out the sink. What business doesn't have a break room sink often stacked with lipstick-rimmed coffee cups and food-encrusted plates? Some days you probably wonder if anyone honors the "Clean up after yourself" rule anymore. No one wants to take on the office sink: They all think it's someone else's problem, or that it's beneath them.

A First Mate, seeing the mess, just rolls up his sleeves and grabs a sponge. (And the bravest of this breed may even tackle the spattered walls of the microwave or the unspeakable collection of smells and cultures emanating from the office fridge.)

Once you've found your own perfect First Mate, you may think the forecast calls for nothing but sunny skies. Not so fast, bud! Even First Mates need a little maintenance. They may give and give, but they also need to receive every now and again. What does this mean? Communicate with your First Mate in a supportive way. Ask him, every day, how he is doing. Celebrate his birthday. Give him some tickets to the ball game or a show. Let him know how important he is to the business.

No one wants to take on the office sink: They think it's someone else's problem, or it's beneath them.

First Mates are so good at giving of themselves, because they truly appreciate what their actions mean to those around them. So just follow their lead, and offer a little support and recognition.

I took my First Mate out to lunch on Secretary's Day – and found a thank-you note on my desk the next morning. Now, I've taken many employees to lunch over the years, but I've never received a thank-you note from any of them.

Sometimes a regular employee won't even *say* "thank you." A First Mate always will.

If your business lacks a First Mate, start looking for one. Just do me a favor: Please don't steal mine.

What If <u>You</u> Are a First Mate?

A genuine First Mate is a rare commodity, so your first concern should be securing a job that makes you happy: a job where your boss values you... where you are welcome to contribute above and beyond your job description... where your talents at fostering cooperation and harmony among others will be of good use.

If your current boss is a jerk, he'll probably stay that way. Is it worth it to sit around waiting for him to change? Probably not. There are better jobs out there, and those businesses will be fortunate to have you. So start looking. (One bit of advice: Look for a manager who values problem-solving skills and independent thinking. If you come across a job where you're just handed an oar and told to row, that's not the place for you.)

Even at the best of jobs, it's wise to keep track of your efforts and contributions for your performance reviews. You might be so stealthy and smooth that your boss doesn't even know how good you are! It's okay to remind him. If he's a good boss, he'll want to know.

So much for the boss. What if your co-workers take advantage of your generosity and willingness to do the dirty work? Figure out how to twist the scenario a little and see if their behavior changes. If you've been stuck with KP duty (to revisit our previous example), try this after getting your boss's okay: Announce that it looks like everyone prefers for one person to clean up the kitchen everyday; then show them a neat little sign-up sheet for kitchen duty with your name at the top of the list for the first week.

Your fellow workers will grumble to themselves, knowing full well they don't want the chore. Odds are they'll say they have an even better idea: Have everyone clean their own items! Now it's <u>their</u> idea to clean up their own messes. So, you volunteer to dispose of anything left. Since everyone has said they'll clean up their own things, anything left must belong to people no longer with the business and can be thrown out.

Of course you can pull this off! A First Mate is clever like a fox – a nice, kindly fox. Besides, if they're all acting like barnyard animals....

In the end, your personality gifts are a wonderful thing. You might not recognize it, but just you <u>being you</u> makes everyone around you better. The lazy will work a little more, the egotistical will occasionally think of others, and the complainers will vent somewhat less. You're a great asset to have at any business!

CHAPTER SIX

The Crew Member

Ships of war, ships of commerce, ships of pleasure... Whatever the craft, Crew Members comprised the majority of the men and women on every ship that has sailed the seven seas. Outcasts, adventurers, prisoners sentenced to a life at sea, regular folks just looking for work... However they entered the trade, they all became Crew Members assigned a specific task: row the oars, hoist the sails, shovel the coal, swab the decks.

And on some of the rougher vessels (read: pirate ships), they'd better do it well. Torturous punishment or death awaited any who gave grief to the Captain. A job well done meant you could have dinner that night, with an occasional pillage and plunder for dessert.

By definition, all but the smallest of businesses have their share of Crew Members, too. They are the engines of the good ship *Enterprise*, the ones who actually *do* the work. They don't discover it, define it, manage it, sell it, or evaluate the work. They just do it. And, in general, they do it because it brings in a steady paycheck. Sure, they might enjoy the social aspects of their work environment, or like the particular product or service a business provides. But, like their seafaring counterparts before them, they mostly work for the pay.

And, in fact, honest work in exchange for fair pay is all many businesses are looking for when hiring most of their employees. Whether a company manufactures cars, caramel corn, or Kleenex, Crew Members willing and able to do their assigned tasks eight to five, Monday through Friday, 50 weeks a year, are essential. Crew Members understand what the company needs from them. Consider the telephone operator who says, "Good morning, XYZ Enterprises. How may I direct your call?" every 10 seconds – for years at a time. Not a particularly challenging job, but one necessary to the smooth operation of the ship. Crew Members view themselves as part of a team and are willing to contribute by working as hard as the next guy.

Crew Members think that if they do the same job this year as last year, they deserve a promotion or raise.

The flip side of this is that the typical Crew Member is *only* willing to work as hard as the next guy. Although they are dependable, dedicated, honest, and efficient, Crew Members are not usually ambitious. They are very aware of what is fair, and, by their definition, consistency is fairness. When some Crew Members receive different treatment, the others are resentful.

Everyone is equal in the eyes of a Crew Member. If the workday ends at 5:00 p.m., everyone leaves at 5:00 p.m. If some employees take long breaks, everyone is entitled to long breaks. If one worker gets to slack off, they all get to slack off. If they receive two weeks of vacation a year, they will take the full two weeks off. If someone takes a sick day to tend to a sick child, others should be able to take time off even if they don't have children themselves. Crew Members wash their own coffee cups, but not the other dirty ones in the sink. They do what they are asked, and little more.

Crew Members also believe promotions and raises should be based on years of work and seniority. Like many business owners and managers, I struggle with this idea. Shouldn't promotions and raises be given for accomplishments? When you were in the second grade, you studied second-grade arithmetic, second-grade social studies, and second-grade science. If you did well, you moved on to the third grade. (In the days before education bureaucrats invented "social promotions," that is.) In the third grade, you studied third-grade arithmetic, third-grade social studies, and third-grade science.

During your school years, promotions came in exchange for your success at progressively difficult activities. No one would think it a good idea to reward a second grader with a *repeat* of the second grade. Successive accomplishments earn you greater rewards.

Yet many Crew Members think that if they do the same job this year as last year, they deserve a promotion or raise. They expect to be rewarded over and over again for the same task. Government workers and union members aside, the real power of promotion in our economic system lies within the individual. Only we can decide to improve our own skills, training, and education – which means that we alone are capable of promoting ourselves into a position where we deserve a better job with greater pay. To hope your employer will automatically grant you a brighter future without your earning it takes away an important part of the human spirit: the part that says you possess the potential within you now. You just have to recognize that potential and act on it.

Governments can just raise taxes when they need more money. The private sector isn't so flexible: Businesses can't just raise their prices on a whim. Businesses deal with the cost of goods sold, overhead, labor, and, most importantly, with the competition. Management balances costs with the market prices of their goods and services just as carefully as the Navigator and Captain watch the winds and trim the sails. Unprofitable times, even failure, are often just a tack away.

Most Crew Members do not understand the fine economic balance required to keep the ship afloat and on course. From their point of view, anniversary raises are to be expected: "My company occupies a big building. We make a lot of stuff. I'm older now, so they should pay me more. They can afford it!" Many Crew Members feel they should be allowed to do second-grade work, year after year, yet be paid as if they're in high school.

Rough seas await managers who don't handle this issue well. Unfortunately, those who seek to avoid conflict or hurt feelings often grant anniversary raises to Crew Members who are simply "good enough." I've spoken with many such managers now stuck with vastly overpaid employees. And they have no idea what to do with them! They agonize about the bottom-line impact of a $60,000-a-year receptionist in a $30,000-a-year market. They fret about the effect on morale if the news gets out about the degree of pay discrepancies. They bemoan the fact that other employees will demand similar compensation.

A small problem is now a very big one. And many times, they further compound that big problem by handling it poorly. Perhaps the $60,000 receptionist is promoted to a position of greater responsibility, where she fails and is fired. Or management hauls out the ever popular, "Times are bad now, and we have to let you go" excuse. Both are messy ways to end an employer-employee relationship. They are unfair to the worker in question, and they do little to instill confidence in the rest of the crew.

A much better method of dealing with your Crew Members' pay expectations is to have their job responsibilities clearly defined in writing. When left to memory, details tend to get edited to the favor of each individual involved. Written documentation of responsibilities that both the Crew Member and his manager agreed to will be the same a year or two later.

Crew Members don't understand the economic balance required to keep the ship afloat and on course.

When a Crew Member feels entitled to a raise, his manager can amend his job description to reflect the new position. New work, new responsibilities, and new risk equals new pay. Both Crew Member and manager should now be able to agree that compensation is not about anniversaries. It's about the work. Sounds like a perfectly logical scenario with which both sides can be comfortable.

But watch out! We're dealing with Crew Members here. These folks usually agree to take on greater responsibility for more pay; however, they may not actually want the work. This reluctance is not always intentional, or even conscious. Human beings are wired to admire achievement and growth, but we're also naturally risk-averse. The result is that many of us hope for praise but are unwilling to take a chance or make the investment to earn it. I couldn't count how many times I've seen good promotion opportunities fall apart. An employee's head bobs an eager "yes," and inside his heart is sinking with a "no." Yes to the pay, no to the work.

I'm reminded of Stan, the owner of a print shop my firm used for many years, and his struggles with a valuable member of his crew. Adam, a pressman with the shop for more than 10 years, was a good and efficient craftsman. The problems began the day Adam decided he deserved more pay because he had "been there" for such a long time. As a non-union shop, Stan's company paid its pressmen at Adam's skill level the current market rate of roughly $18.00 an hour. Paying someone in Adam's position a higher wage would mean passing the cost on to customers. In our highly competitive market, Stan would have lost some business.

> **Many of us hope for praise but are unwilling to take a chance or make the investment to earn it.**

Stan considered Adam's position – his years of good, honest work and his loyalty to the company – and came up with what he hoped would be an acceptable solution: a promotion to night-shift supervisor. The additional responsibilities of the job (Adam would supervise a crew of five, while continuing to operate the press he ran during his old day shift) came with a decent raise of $6.00 more an hour in pay. The pressman accepted.

Calm seas for a month or so.... Then late one afternoon, as their shifts overlapped, Adam asked to speak with Stan. Turns out he didn't like the new job.

It was difficult to manage the crew at night. They took long smoking breaks. They argued among themselves, disrupting others. They skipped work or called in sick without enough notice to reschedule jobs. Bottom line, Adam

> **Crew Members' Talents**
> - They are dependable.
> - They are accurate and consistent.
> - They are honest.
> - They will do their assigned tasks well.
> - They can be quite experienced in their chosen fields.
> - They usually treat their jobs with respect.
> - They are fair with others.
> - They can be quite loyal.
> - They manage their own time well.
> - They like identifying themselves as part of a team.
>
> **Crew Members' Drawbacks**
> - They are not usually ambitious and will avoid major career moves.
> - They do not usually have breakthrough ideas.
> - They may have difficulty resolving conflicts with their co-workers.
> - They may allow personal problems to interfere with work.
> - They are hesitant to critique a co-worker's poor work habits in a constructive manner.
> - They will rely on managers to deal with poor workers.
> - They may not take the initiative to further their own education and training.
> - They can be highly inflexible.
> - They don't usually volunteer for tasks outside their assigned job functions.

wanted his old job back. Not wanting to lose a good employee and skilled pressman, Stan agreed. He gave the pressman his old job back – at his old salary.

To say Adam was unhappy is an understatement. He was incensed! How dare Stan cut his pay! "I've worked here for 10 years! I should get a raise!" Stan reminded him that the raise was for the new job. No new job, no raise. Adam reminded Stan that he'd worked there for *10 years*. He threatened to quit. Undaunted, Stan pointed out that the going rate for pressmen operating Adam's type of equipment was, in fact, about $18.00 an hour. In the end, Adam quit. A successful decade-old business relationship ended.

Stan was sorry to lose such a skilled employee, but the greater loss was Adam's: The pressman failed to see that his earning power was in his own hands. The promotion to night-shift supervisor was not just about a $6.00-an-hour raise. It offered him an opportunity to redefine his role, to learn something new, and to elevate his position within the business. Who knows? A promotion to supervisor might have been Adam's first step into management, a new career opportunity in the middle of his 30- to 40-year working life.

My colleague's issue with Adam was not that the pressman was lazy or inept or dishonest. Adam simply did not understand one of the fundamental economic principles behind the operation of a business, *any* business. Just as a ship is not built to sit in dry dock, a business does not exist to provide employment for a crew.

This lack of understanding crops up in Crew Members of all personality types and backgrounds. The office social butterfly is particularly prone to it. Fun to have around, social butterflies such as a bright young woman who worked for me some years ago are also destructive to a business's health. Intelligent, talented, and spirited, Janet spent 90 percent of her time productively. My biggest challenge was trying to figure out when that time was.

How often I passed Janet's work area only to hear her on a personal phone call (the breathless exclamations of "Then what did he do?!" and "Oh, my gosh!" were the giveaway). After I had confirmed that the calls were more than occasional events, I whispered that I'd like to talk with her. (I had to whisper. She was on the phone.) Once she was in my office, I acknowledged that we all need to take or make personal calls at times, but that hers seemed quite lengthy. In fact, I added, they were affecting the accuracy of her work.

> **Just as a ship is not built to sit in dry dock, a business does not exist to provide employment for a crew.**

Her response was that I owed her an apology for interfering with her personal life. "I am indeed interfering," I said, resisting the urge to grab her Starbucks venti caramel mocha and dump the steaming, gooey mess over her head. "I am trying to separate your work time from your personal time." Our clients, I reminded her, pay us to give our full attention to their needs.

Well aware I was not getting through to this young woman, I tried to come up with an analogy to clarify things: "Imagine you're meeting with an attorney. You pay him $300 an hour for his expertise. Yet while you're telling him about your legal needs, the attorney is on the phone talking to a golf buddy about the round they played last weekend." Janet retorted, "That's *completely* different!" Two weeks later, she quit, unwilling or incapable of changing her behavior or her attitude.

Like many Crew Members, the Adams and Janets of the world are not looking for careers – or for excitement, advancement, or change. They are looking for jobs: a reasonable amount of effort for a reasonable paycheck. If the work is interesting, fine. More important, however, are security, a regular paycheck, and to be treated "fairly." Crew Members' lives are outside of work. Their interests – their passions even – lie in hobbies, friends, families, religion, sports, or maybe just their next meals... but definitely not in their jobs.

Provide your Crew Members with the security and stability they seek, and you'll have good workers.

It is the responsibility of anyone managing Crew Members to realize this difference. A successful manager recognizes the limits of most Crew Members' career aspirations and is comfortable with them. Push past that line, and everyone is heading for the lifeboats!

To modern-day Explorers, Navigators, Captains, and First Mates, Crew Members can be a real puzzle. "Why does he settle for that accounting clerk position? He could've passed his CPA exam years ago." "Why didn't she apply for the office manager job when it opened up? She can't *really* be happy as just another receptionist."

Ever catch yourself saying something like this? How easily we project our own ambitions onto others, only to be surprised when we learn they're quite content with their place on the boat. (Back when real-life Crew Members were often convicts or conscripts considered expendable and with no prospect for advancement, the bosses probably didn't spend much time on such questions.)

Hard-working but not ambitious... dependable but inflexible... honest but not overly creative. It is not being critical of your employees to recognize that many of them, perhaps the majority, exhibit typical Crew Member traits. It is realistic. Like the old "too many cooks in the kitchen" analogy, your ship of commerce won't sail far if everyone is fighting for control of the helm.

Crew Members are essential to a successful voyage – but managers must recognize that their job expectations are completely different from those of an Explorer, a Navigator, a Captain, or a First Mate. Provide your Crew Members with the security and stability they seek, and you'll have good workers. But push them too far, expose them to risk, or ask too much, and, like Adam and Janet, they'll be swimming back to shore.

What If <u>You</u> Are a Crew Member?

First, determine whether you truly are "just" a Crew Member! If you start working at age 20 and retire at 65, that's 45 years of labor. With an eight-hour day and a two-week annual vacation, that 45-year period adds up to 90,000 hours of work. What do you want to become with all that time? Well, many Crew Members just want to get paid.

Some years ago, when the California lottery had an unusually high prize, everyone in my office chipped in a buck to purchase a number of tickets. Curious what kind of life each would choose were we all to win, I asked the group. I can still hear one employee, Jeff, proclaiming, "I'll <u>definitely</u> quit. I'll never have to work again!"

Now, consider that each person's winning share would have been about $40,000 a year – enough to make you comfortable, but certainly not wealthy, especially in California. Yet Jeff's driving thought was never to work again. Food in the fridge, gas in the car, and a nice, predictable life… that represented his perfect world. Other staff members would have used the opportunity to expand their horizons a little. Some said they'd continue to work, but in a more entertaining field. A few mentioned starting their own businesses. Jeff, a Crew Member to the core, saw no need for a job if he had no need for income.

So, what would <u>you</u> do?! If you found yourself independently wealthy tomorrow, would you keep your current job, go back to school, start that business you've dreamed of, travel the world…? In fact, any answer other than Jeff's means that there's a little bit of an Explorer, Navigator, or Captain in you. Why not try tapping into that side of your personality now?

CHAPTER SEVEN

The Stowaway

Ah, the Stowaway. I wish I didn't have to write this chapter. The crews on ships of exploration once had to deal with plague-infested rats in the cargo hold, scuttling stowaways that ate away at the core of their vessels and contaminated everyone they touched. Stowaways in the business world can be just as damaging to operations and morale. The faster you rid your ship of them, the better off you'll be.

So what exactly is a Stowaway, you're probably wondering – and do I have any hiding among my own crew?! A Stowaway is an employee who wants a free ride at your expense. "I don't get paid enough to work hard" and "This job stinks, but I need the money" are typical Stowaway justifications for their laziness.

Underneath these casual words, however, is a fierce determination to do as little work as possible for the most amount of pay. When the scale fully tips in his favor, the Stowaway feels as if he's "won." A Stowaway's relationship with his employer is always adversarial: One side must lose if the other is to win. The Stowaway will always structure the job so he comes out on top.

How do Stowaways get on board, you ask? Can't I just stop them at the dock? Tough to do! Stowaways are masters of disguise. Always clever, and often quite intelligent, Stowaways will tell you exactly what you want to hear in order to get the job. Some of the most unrepentant Stowaways I've met had thoroughly impressed me during the interview process (just weeks or months earlier) with their enthusiasm, ideas, or abilities. But run across enough Stowaways during a few decades in business, and you'll start to recognize the signs....

> **Selfishness is the Stowaway's core personality trait, which explains why they are such inflexible workers.**

Experience has taught me that Stowaways share certain characteristics; for example, their work histories tend to follow similar paths. After college, they gravitate to the "party" jobs – bartender, ski instructor, lifeguard – or head off for the ever-popular "year of travel." "If I have to work, it had better be fun" is the Stowaway's motto.

The whole notion that "one's labor creates value for a business that, in exchange, pays you for your time" is utterly foreign to these folks. I once heard a Stowaway share with a co-worker that, "My favorite job is not working." Needless to say, her eight-year career bouncing from job to job as a cocktail waitress hadn't prepared her for the responsibilities of a traditional office setting.

Of course, millions of people working these "fun" jobs are indeed dedicated, industrious, and loyal workers. I too worked in the restaurant business at one point, and tried to get a stint as a lifeguard as well. (I loved to surf and thought I was great at it, but not all of my water skills were quite as good. Who'd have thought swimming was so important for the task of lifesaving?) I'm referring here specifically to those people who seek only their own pleasure and comfort while on the job and who couldn't care less about adding value to the workplace or furthering their employers' goals.

Supreme selfishness, in fact, is the Stowaway's core personality trait, which explains why they are such highly inflexible workers. Stowaways resist anything that creates value for their host organization or its customers – such as change, compromise, or cooperation, all concepts anathema to these self-centered beings. Anything that threatens to dislodge a Stowaway from his place at the center of the universe doesn't stand a chance. If asked to stay late, a Stowaway's rolling eyes signal how much he'd rather not. Show a Stowaway that his work is unacceptable, and he'll respond with a teenage sigh so loud his co-workers raise their heads from their tasks.

I've found Stowaways lurking on my own little ship several times. It's still painful to recall the energy I wasted struggling to convert them into Crew Members. Fortunately, not all Stowaways hide out for long.

Some years back, I hired a young woman as our new receptionist. As at many smaller companies, the receptionist plays a central role in the smooth operation of our business. Responsibilities include arriving first to open up the office and having a reliable car for running errands. Cathy agreed to the terms, and we decided she'd begin the following Monday morning at 8:00.

ALL HANDS ON DECK

Monday morning I arrived at 8:10 to find the office locked and dark. Ten minutes later, someone dropped Cathy off for work. I reminded her that she needed to be at the office at 8:00 with her own vehicle. Sure, sure, no problem. We moved on with the day.

On Tuesday, Cathy didn't arrive until 8:30. Apparently her morning schedule included driving her boyfriend to his job before coming into the office. I asked whether this young man had a car of his own. "Yes, but I like to drive his car because it's so much cooler than mine." I reminded Cathy that I needed her *here* at work *with a car* at eight sharp. Okay, okay. Message received – or so I thought, until she showed up Wednesday at 8:15.

I asked whether anything was preventing her from doing her job. Nope. All right, let's see how the rest of the week turns out. Perhaps there's a chance to save this little pound puppy. She was fairly young, so maybe she just had a few poor habits. A week or two at Warner Design Basic Training might give her some sea legs and turn her around.

Well, Thursday morning arrived without Cathy. At 9:00, she called to inform me: "I've got to quit my job because I'm moving back up to Pasadena to live with my parents because I'm best friends with my mom and we love to shop together and the parties are much cooler there than in San Diego." And, yes, her words burst through the phone in one breathless sentence just like that.

Lesson learned: A tendency to bend the rules and refusing to conform are signs of real trouble ahead – signs as serious as those red flags warning sailors of gale force winds beyond the safety of a harbor.

Would you believe Cathy doesn't hold the record for the shortest stay aboard my ship? That honor goes to a young would-be Stowaway named Greg.

Greg came to me with a resume that featured many of what I eventually learned to recognize as Stowaway warning signs. Brief stints as bartender and construction worker checkered his work history. After deciding he wanted to be a graphic designer, he had enrolled in the quickest trade-school program he could find. (Another warning sign: Many such schools promise exciting, lucrative careers. Yet they don't always provide enough training to qualify students for those promised careers – nor do their "get 'em in, get 'em out" program schedules give students time to realize they may not be suited to the field.)

> **Lesson learned: A tendency to bend the rules and refusing to conform are signs of real trouble ahead.**

After completing his studies, Greg took a job at the same school. Twelve months later he was ready to move on, because the school wouldn't give him a raise. Swayed by his verbal skills and energy, I decided to hire him.

Standard policy at my firm places new hires in support roles for five or six months, so we can evaluate their work quality and skills. Three hours into his first day on the job, Greg entered my office hoping to discuss his career goals.

Impressed with his obvious ambition, I suggested he put his goals down in writing so we'd have something concrete to discuss. (This puts the responsibility for developing a plan on the employee's shoulders.) I expected to talk again in a few weeks, after he had the opportunity to see how he was settling in.

Next morning in walked Greg with his plan. Surprised again by his ambition, I asked when he would like to talk. "How about this morning?" he suggested. We set a 10:00 appointment. Greg arrived promptly and, taking a seat, slipped a sheet of paper across my desk. The document outlined a three-point plan:

Goal #1: To create award-winning print and broadcast ads.
Goal #2: To take on *pro bono* work for national charities.
Goal #3: To earn a salary double his current income.

Greg's timeframe? One to two years.

I was flabbergasted at how unrealistic his aspirations were. As an entry-level designer, Greg's skills were adequate but far from outstanding. A single year of design experience left him at least a dozen shy of where he apparently thought his skills were.

Addressing his first goal, I pointed out that our firm was not an advertising agency – especially not one that did any type of broadcasting work. I mentioned that, during his interview, I had shared the firm's portfolio with him and described in detail the type of work we do. Regarding the second goal, I reminded him that *pro bono* means "for free" in Latin. As a small-business owner, I explained, I can't afford to pay people to work for free. I added that many of my designers do indeed engage in *pro bono* work on their own time and away from the office.

Before he departed, this Stowaway left his manifesto displayed on his computer as a final act of bravado.

As for the third goal – to double his salary in about 18 months – I was a little harsher. I asked first whether he thought the idea was realistic in *any* industry? No comment. Turning to our own industry, I tried to offer him a fairly realistic scenario: With a good deal of additional experience, a few lucky breaks, and a great economy, he could double his salary in six to 10 years (assuming he was as talented as he professed).

Greg looked calmly across the desk at me and said, "I thought so." I asked him, "Where does this leave us? Is today your last day?" "Yep."

An hour later, he was out the door. Before he departed, however, this Stowaway left his manifesto prominently displayed on his computer screen as a final act of bravado. Two different designers came to tell me and then commiserate about this odd behavior. Yet Greg's strange behavior was classic Stowaway: They need gratification, and they need it now. As the center of his universe, the Stowaway sees no reason to dally. If a job doesn't please him, he's usually gone in a flash.

Not all Stowaways skim blithely across the sea's surface like Greg did. Some lie far, far below. Stealthy submarines of the workplace, their true natures remain hidden for a time. Their work seems adequate, but closer inspection reveals that it's actually below average. They aim to ride along on your ship without touching an oar.

Always on the lookout for half-work at full pay, this variety of Stowaway might be the one who always volunteers to run errands at your office. Twenty-minute jaunts that take two hours... mumbled references to bad traffic... Sound familiar? Like all Stowaways, these folks have no intention of paying full fare for passage on your ship. They sneak on, hide out in the shadows, and jump off as soon as they're discovered.

I once hired a submariner Stowaway named Mark, recommended by a vendor we'd used for some time. Mark's portfolio demonstrated work of good quality, and he claimed his computer skills were "excellent." I anticipated that he would be a good addition to the crew.

Smooth sailing, at first. Then, on Valentine's Day, Mark didn't show up for work. At 10:00, we called his house but

Stowaways' Talents
- They are clever.
- They are often quite intelligent.
- They will do their assigned tasks when told.
- They are interesting (in a way).

Stowaways' Drawbacks
- They only look out for themselves.
- They don't feel they must work to create opportunities.
- They don't usually have breakthrough ideas.
- They may have difficulty resolving personal conflicts with co-workers.
- They will often openly criticize their co-workers.
- They will hide their lack of skills from managers.
- They won't usually take any initiative.
- They are highly inflexible.
- They don't usually volunteer for tasks outside their assigned job functions (except for errands that take them away from the office, of course).
- They are undependable.
- They are disloyal and often dishonest.
- They tend to use other people.
- They can create chaos.
- They are trouble!

no one answered. Mark sauntered in about an hour later. Everyone had been worried about him, so I asked if everything was okay. "I'm fine," he said, "but it's Valentine's Day, and I had to give my girlfriend some flowers."

"That's nice. But we've been worried about you for over two hours. Valentine's Day can be a very special event, but you need to take care of it before or after work."

Mark actually looked puzzled at my words, as if my viewpoint was foreign to him. There you go – that should have been my first clue we had a Stowaway aboard! Mark actually thought his response to my enquiries was appropriate.

> **His father had taught him it's okay to lie to get a job, because you can develop the skills needed later.**

As the center of the universe, why shouldn't an employee come and go as he chooses? Being Number One in importance, everyone else, including bosses, coworkers, and customers, comes second.

As another few weeks passed, I noticed Mark was much less efficient than his co-workers. "Excellent" did not describe his computer skills at all, I concluded after closer inspection. His skills were downright primitive. Mark clearly had little training, much less experience, using the design software with which he had claimed great proficiency. I was stunned and told him he couldn't stay on at the firm.

I then asked why he lied during the interview. His father, he explained, had taught him it's okay to lie to get a job, because you can always develop the skills needed later. I've always wondered what else Mark had lied about, or what he's lying about these days. Most Stowaways are never wrong. They are singularly cursed with a seemingly endless list of poor parents, inept teachers, unfair bosses, mean co-workers, and backstabbing friends.

The plank is the quickest way to deal with these troublemakers. Get them off your ship as fast as possible. Prepare the way for a quick exodus by requiring probationary periods for all new hires (after checking with your attorney about applicable labor codes). If a new hire's performance is not what you expected, you want the ability to part company with as few hassles as possible.

An extra word of caution on this subject: It is always important to have every "I" dotted and "T" crossed when preparing to fire someone, but especially when that worker is a Stowaway. With your paperwork shipshape before you confront a Stowaway, he'll probably go away quietly (and you can get back to running your business). Unfortunately, when Stowaways are cornered, the fight may turn nasty. In fact, some Stowaways plan their legal battles from the start. Evaluate a Stowaway's work as unacceptable and begin the severance process, and shrieks of "You don't like me!" or "You discriminate against [fill in the blank]!" fill the air. Have a good lawyer ready, and deal with it quickly. Your crew is watching.

> **Determined to see the Antarctic at any cost, Blackborow smuggled himself aboard the Endurance.**

Rehabilitating a Stowaway is almost impossible. I've never seen it happen. Those discovered aboard my ship were all too ready to leave when confronted. Like rats in the cargo hold, they scurry off as soon as light shines on them. Once you discover a Stowaway, be honest with yourself about the chances of changing that person – because you can't.

They can only change themselves. And why should they? It's easier to find a new hideout.

Most Stowaways board a ship with so much baggage that change is very difficult. Heck, change is difficult for most of us, so imagine if you're burdened with dysfunctional personality traits ingrained over a lifetime. Stowaways may have learned from childhood how to lie, cheat, and steal. Cutting corners, avoiding responsibility, and undermining co-workers – perhaps smiling to the boss's face all the while – are as natural to Stowaways as breathing.

A Stowaway's poor habits are not always severe offenses, but they will gradually poison your workplace. As they observe what the Stowaway gets away with, other workers often (consciously or not) modify their own good traits after those of the Stowaway.

Every rule has its exception, of course – and one of the greatest exploration stories of all time offers just such an example. In 1914, Sir Ernest Shackleton set off for Antarctica in the *Endurance* with a crew of 26. Stopping in Buenos Aires, the legendary explorer interviewed several sailors to replace three he'd just been forced to sack. A 19-year-old Welshman, Perce Blackborow, was among the hopefuls, but Shackleton turned him down because of his youth and inexperience.

Determined to see the Antarctic at any cost, Blackborow smuggled himself aboard the *Endurance* and hid in a locker, eating what scraps two pals in on the secret could sneak down to him. Three days out of port, he was discovered. Hauled before Shackleton, the defiant Stowaway felt the force of the captain's ire and irritation – and was then given the job of steward, assisting the ship's cook. The position came with a single caveat: Should the voyagers' situation become dire, Shackleton told him, "If anyone has to be eaten, then *you* will be the first."

Fortunately for our young hero, the only thing he lost on the voyage were his toes (from frostbite), not his life when the food rations dwindled. Not only did Blackborow overcome his inauspicious start by earning a reputation as one of the hardest-working members of the *Endurance* crew, Shackleton gave him the honor of being the first person in history to set foot on the forboding ice fortress known as Antarctica's Elephant Island.

The tale of Perce Blackborow teaches us two important lessons about Stowaways. First, that on a very rare occasion you may meet one who can actually be turned into a valuable Crew Member. And second, had the steward ended up the one in the dinner pot, rather than the one cooking with it, his fate would prove my theory that Stowaways are usually their own worst enemies.

What If You Are a Stowaway?

An unrepentant Stowaway wouldn't be reading this book, so there's hope yet! If you are indeed repentant, today is the day to begin the new you! Take a long, appraising look in the mirror. Be honest about whether you like what you see. If the reflection displeases you, what can you do to fix it? Only you can correct your bad habits. Sure, change is difficult, but what other options do you have? You can do it!

CHAPTER EIGHT

Assembling Your Crew

By now, I'm sure you've developed a clear picture of how many Explorers, Navigators, Captains, First Mates, and Crew Members man your ship. And, if the only concrete result of this ongoing analysis is that you've spotted any Stowaways lurking in the shadows, you're still far ahead! Just remember: If you did find Stowaways, *today* is the day to deal with them. Go ahead and try converting them to Crew Members. (It's unlikely, but you could be harboring the next Perce Blackborow.) Put measurable criteria for their future evaluations in writing. If they come up to the mark, great. If not, show 'em the plank.

As for the other shipboard personalities, how many of each do you need? Many smaller businesses begin with just an Explorer and a Navigator, an idea person and a guide. One partner's strengths cover the other's weaknesses, and vice versa. I once worked with an architectural firm that had three founding partners: an artistic visionary, a business manager, and a salesperson. Such partnerships work well as long as each founder sticks with his appointed job. At some point, though, success requires growth: Crew Members, someone to oversee them, and, if you're fortunate, a First Mate somewhere in the mix.

Large corporations need many of each type, although the majority will still be Crew Members. IBM surely has many thousands of Explorers, Navigators, and Captains overseeing each international operation, each division, and each department within a division. A fast-food franchise, on the other hand, is part of a corporation but has no need for an Explorer or Navigator. The franchise founder was the Explorer; the franchise developer was the Navigator. Such enterprises require just a Captain (the restaurant manager), a First Mate (the assistant managers), and Crew Members (the cooks and counter staff). The parent company handles the rest.

> **Let's start with the Stowaway, the one character you don't want on board under any circumstances.**

Whether you've just launched a business (or been promoted to department head) and are preparing for your first trip out of port – or your vessel has been seaworthy for some time and you just need more hands on deck – the rules for assembling the best crew possible are the same.

Let's start with the Stowaway, the one character you don't want on board under any circumstances. As the most self-serving and self-centered individuals you'll interview, they should be the easiest to spot now that you know what to watch out for.

When advertising for a new graphic designer, for example, I specify that applicants mail me their resumes and samples of their work. This allows me to check several things, most importantly whether or not the applicant can follow directions. Did he actually mail the materials, as stated in the ad? Or, did he do what was most convenient for him and send the materials by e-mail or fax? I need designers who can follow directions. Bending small rules before you even set foot on the ship suggests more serious problems once we cast off.

Having clean copies of an applicant's work ahead of time also allows me to check for typographical errors. Employees at my firm work with type all day long. I can't afford designers who cannot spell. Whatever your business, even a simple cover letter can reveal volumes about an applicant's personality and attention to detail. Can you afford a receptionist, salesperson, or division manager who relies on spell check for everything?!

Arriving for the interview on time and dressing appropriately for the particular office are obvious tests for prospective employees in any field. Earthquakes, riots, and accidents that shut down all of I-5 aside, there's no excuse in the age of MapQuest to arrive late for an interview. Missed our appointment? I bet you have an issue with chronic tardiness.

As for attire, every industry is different. T-shirts and jeans are the norm at some graphic design firms; at others (such as mine), a shirt and tie is regulation. A firm's clients dictate the office dress in our industry. A prospective designer wanting to work for us would find that out and dress appropriately. (Besides, no one's going to take points from an applicant for showing up dressed *too* well, right?)

I learned my own lesson about the importance of my crew's appearance the hard way. Years back, before I was so particular about office attire, clients occasionally commented about certain Crew Members' lack of professionalism. In some cases, the criticism was justified: Perhaps the designer treated deadlines more as "guidelines" or had misplaced an original photo. But other times the criticism was not justified. The common denominator, I eventually realized, was that the Crew Members in question were the least dressed up members of the staff. "The customer is king," after all.... So if my clients like ties, I like ties! I want to hire people my clients like, and dressing appropriately is a part of that.

I'm sure you've conducted interviews with someone like John, the prospective Crew Member you'll meet next. The question is whether you recognized him as a Stowaway before he came on board! Both John's resume and work samples impressed me, and his job experience and schooling seemed a good fit. Unfortunately for him, that was the best impression I ever had of the guy.

First, he arrived 10 minutes late to his interview, claiming unfamiliarity with the neighborhood. *Strike one!* What job isn't full of uncertainties?! Even Crew Members on an assembly line can foresee the possibility of machinery parts breaking and be prepared to find a solution. Had John been serious, he'd have scouted the firm's location, noting travel distances and parking options. If a prospective employee doesn't adopt a be-prepared-for-anything approach to the interview, he's sure to be ready with excuses when the work itself presents challenges.

Ushering him into my office, I took note of his outfit: cowboy boots, blue jeans, and a T-shirt. *Strike two!* John was obviously dressed to impress – himself, not me. If he wanted to impress me, he'd have asked the receptionist ahead of time about the dress code (you know, when he called to check on parking). His intent was clearly to establish himself as cool, hip, laid-back, whatever.... All of which reeks of a self-centeredness that promises future conflicts with co-workers and clients.

I asked John to take a seat while I reviewed his portfolio. Slouching down as if he expected me to switch on ESPN rather than my interviewing skills, he placed his right boot on top of his left knee, the scuffed toe poking up past the table's surface. Whoa, cowboy! Are you really going to put that thing on my furniture? It didn't take me long to review his work: The samples accompanying his resume were clearly his best efforts, and the rest only average. Confident I knew enough about his personality and work skills to judge him a poor choice for the job, I thought I'd let him throw the final strike to himself. "Do you have any questions for me?" I asked.

First, he arrived 10 minutes late to his interview, claiming unfamiliarity with the neighborhood. Strike one!

"What kind of cool projects will I be working on here?" he drawled (again focusing on himself). Before I could reply, he added, with slightly more animation, "What's my starting pay and benefits package?" *Strike three!*

Human resource guides usually suggest asking the applicant if he has any questions before concluding an interview. It's only polite to give the other person the chance to ask about your work environment and benefits, right? Pay particular attention to those questions, however: This may be the moment a perfectly attired, punctual applicant reveals her true colors. If every question concerns pay, vacation time, or insurance coverage, beware! That's a good sign she considers the employer-employee relationship a one-way street and is only thinking of herself.

Of course, everyone *wants* to know those details. Mortgages and kids' medical bills don't pay themselves. But a simple query ("I'd like a few details about your benefits package") combined with questions that reflect an interest in adding value to the business ("Where do you see the company in five years – and how can the members of your design team contribute to reaching those goals?") is quite different from an applicant like John who is all "me, me, *me!*" Obviously, John was a Stowaway. Fortunately, I spotted him on the dock.

> **The result is that these reluctant managers tend to hire employees based on personal chemistry.**

Consider the interview like a honeymoon: It can be the best time in the relationship. If, during an interview, you notice the conversation revolving around the candidate's needs and wants – rather than what the two of you have to offer each other – the marriage is already on the rocks. Hire too many workers like that, and your business may be dashed on those same rocks as well.

So much for Stowaways. Rounding out the rest of your Crew can be much more difficult. Tossing out the question, "So, are you more of a Navigator or a First Mate?" doesn't really work in the typical job interview.

It's no secret that small-business owners usually possess limited hiring skills. After all, entrepreneurs go into business because of their talents in event planning or architecture, massage therapy or model train repairs – not because they earned master's degrees in HR management. What is often overlooked is the similar plight many managers at larger organizations often face. I recently came across a young scientist who, after several quick promotions, is now in the position of hiring and managing a sizable staff. As you can imagine, not a lot of the work done for his physics Ph.D. prepared him for this management role. Such situations are repeated throughout corporate America in every industry imaginable.

The result is that these reluctant managers tend to hire employees based on personal chemistry (once an applicant meets the basic qualifications for the job). Extroverts admire people with outgoing personalities. Introverts gravitate to quiet types. Most of us tend to be attracted to people like ourselves. Yet while this natural response makes for enjoyable lunch breaks, it's a serious problem for the business overall. Most companies require a variety of personality types if they truly are to thrive.

Imagine even the smallest of water crafts, crewed only by four or five Explorers: Everyone is running around with grand ideas, but no one has control of the helm. Or a ship full of Crew Members: With each person waiting to be told what to do, the ship stays tied to its moorings for months (until they finally scramble back to the dock and abandon ship). Worse yet, a ship of nothing but Stowaways, each thinking everyone else will do the work. The whole lot of 'em will be headed for Davy Jones' locker when the first storm blows.

So, once I've verified the basics ("Can this person actually *do* the job?"), my goal in any interview is to determine what the applicant is like. Sure, he seems a reliable Crew

Member type, and that's just what I need – but is there a little Explorer in him? Great! I've got a solid design team right now, but it would be nice to throw someone into the mix who'll occasionally walk into my office with a few "crazy" ideas. What if I already have several such Crew Member/Explorers on board though? Then I probably need a designer with some of the leadership traits of a Captain or the organizational skills of a Navigator – someone who can add a little order to the "crazy" ideas the others enjoy tossing about.

If you're looking to fill a new position (say your business or department has grown to the point where you can no longer act as both Navigator and Captain), put your needs in writing before you even begin the application process. List the traits, skills, educational background, training, and work history the ideal person for that job would possess. Keep this list in mind during the interviews, and the shifting currents of personality will be less likely to sway your judgment.

Remember: Your goal is not to hire another "you." You already have one "you" – that's quite enough. You're trying to hire a "them." Whether that individual is an Explorer, Navigator, Captain, or First Mate does not matter. You're looking for the best possible employee for a very specific task, not someone you'd enjoy having a beer with after work.

I may have been doing this for 30 years, but I must still remind myself of the type of person I should be hiring before I begin each and every job interview. It's so easy to get swept away and hire someone simply because you like that person! Let's take a look at some of the questions I use to sift through the employee hopefuls who've made it to the actual interview:

When looking for an Explorer, I ask...
What can you tell me about some of your past successes?
This question jump-starts Explorers like a lit match thrown into gasoline. Genuine Explorers have had many successes. Watch their eyes dart around the room as they enthusiastically recall past glories. Someone without even a trace of Explorer in him will have no idea how to answer this question.

What ideas have you had for new businesses?
This is a natural follow-up to the first question – and those ideas about the future are exactly why you may want this individual on board. Smart Explorers will share their goals with you and point out how your business could benefit from them.

> You're looking for the best possible employee, not just someone you'd enjoy having a beer with after work.

Would having an organized assistant or staff help or hurt your performance?
Experienced Explorers usually admit that they value a good support staff. Someone who says he doesn't need any help is either inexperienced in anything but the smallest business operation or is an egomaniac or a liar.

When you're bored at work, what do you do?
This is a trick question: Genuine Explorers are rarely bored. They are too busy brainstorming, chasing dreams, or making deals. Struggling with boredom at work is the clock watcher's specialty. Explorers usually want more time for work, not less.

When looking for a Navigator, I ask...
What business ideas do you wish you'd thought of?
Excellent trend-spotters, Navigators usually have good answers to this query. The examples they offer won't always be in your specific industry, but they will exemplify the applicants' ability to make astute observations. When considering your candidates, remember that Navigators are never the first ones to take on huge risk. Their talents lie in spotting new currents on the high seas of the business world and determining how to take advantage of them.

How do you rate yourself on perseverance?
True Navigators will say they're quite perseverant and have long attention spans. Focused on the long-term goal rather than the short haul, Navigators don't need to be humored or gratified quickly. An honest "non-Navigator" will admit he prefers a fast-paced, exciting work environment, or perhaps the quiet comfort of a predictable job in which little changes from day to day and a long-range outlook is not required.

> **Every day brings new challenges, so the ability to shift gears willingly and with little warning is important.**

How do you feel about working on someone else's ideas?
Navigators often say they enjoy the "process" of a work project and frequently use a puzzle analogy to answer this question: "Even if I didn't come up with the project, I enjoy the puzzle of solving it." Navigators love to understand systems – how to simplify them and come up with the correct outcome. They know they're part of a team and are comfortable working within that framework.

How do you increase your business knowledge after work?
Navigators know they don't know it all. They will read

books and magazines, watch educational programs, visit museums, attend lectures, take classes – all on their own time. Navigators don't wait for their employers to send them out for extra training. They know what they need for *their* own futures and will go get it.

When looking for a Captain, I ask…
How do you feel when responsible for leading a group?
Conscientious and dependable, good Captains take their parental roles seriously. They are mature enough to accept the fact that any ship must weather rough seas in between periods of calm progress. Some are quiet and analytic; others are outgoing and social. But all exude confidence in their ability to lead.

How comfortable are you with switching tasks?
The correct answer here is "very." Every day brings new challenges, so the ability to shift gears willingly and with little warning is important. You don't want a Captain who can't supervise a variety of employees and projects. And a Captain who prefers completing one task before beginning another won't be much good when the hull springs a leak at the same time the boom knocks half your new recruits into the drink.

How are your math and record-keeping skills?
The boss must be able to evaluate what's working and what is not, which products or services to drop and which to expand. Meticulous record-keeping and a thorough understanding of the company ledger is a must.

When you notice a personnel conflict, what do you do?
The answer you want to hear is: "Resolve it." You don't want a Captain who's afraid to deal with conflict or who

hopes time will take care of a problem. What good parent lets a two-year-old repeatedly burn his hand on the stovetop in the hope that, with time, the child will learn?

When looking for a First Mate, I ask...
How well do you get along with strangers?
First Mates know how to get along with almost anyone. Neither shy nor loudmouthed, they can handle pretty much anyone who walks through your front door. Always professional and courteous, First Mates know how to talk as well as to listen.

When asked to multitask, how do you feel?
First Mates are usually candid, so to answer this question they'll share how they've successfully handled simultaneous projects in the past. My First Mate can acknowledge the mailman with a nod or signature, converse on the phone, and review accounts receivable at the same time. Smiling all the while, of course.

What jobs would you refuse to do?
Most First Mates will pause at this question, never having thought about it before. Their first reaction is usually "None" (sometimes qualified by saying they draw the line at anything illegal or immoral, but that's obviously a reasonable caveat). Some candidates may even get a chuckle out of the question. A First Mate does whatever needs to be done, after all!

It's 5:00 p.m., and a co-worker asks you for a little help. What would you do?
"Help him" is the answer you want to hear. What else would a genuine First Mate do? A "non-First Mate" would ask for some qualifications to the initial request: "What do

you need?" "How long will it take?" "Does it have to be done now?" You see, this person is looking for an out. True First Mates are always willing to lend a hand if it keeps the vessel on course and out of harm's way.

When looking for a Crew Member, I ask...
Do you believe in a fair day's work for a fair day's pay?
Crew Members will identify with this statement; it's how they're wired. Now, they may ask you what you mean by "fair," which gives you a good opportunity to bring up the topic of their goals. Most Crew Members, however, are comfortable with a "fair deal" because they want a job in which the employer-employee relationship is clearly spelled out: Exactly how many hours do they work, what do they earn, what are their days off?

> **True First Mates are always willing to lend a hand if it keeps the vessel on course and out of harm's way.**

If something needs to be done and the task is not usually your responsibility, would you do it anyway? Or would you say that whoever's supposed to do it should take care of it?
A Crew Member with no spark of First Mate in him will respond, "The person who's supposed to do it should be the one doing it." After all, this question gets back to the Crew Member's "fairness" doctrine: "Only ask me to do things I'm supposed to do. I don't have to do anything beyond what's in my job description. Don't force me to be what I'm not, or make me do things I find uncomfortable. That's not fair."

What's your favorite day of the week?
This one puzzles most Crew Members. They worry that if they say the wrong day, they won't get hired. But a straightforward Crew Member – one willing to tell you

what he thinks, rather than what he thinks you want to hear – will say "Saturday" or "Sunday" (and then proceed to tell you about a hobby or interest outside of work). It's only fair that those days are "their" days, because they've had to split the other ones with you. This is a completely understandable attitude, so the answer is not an inappropriate one for Crew Members.

But beware the lurking Stowaway! Stowaways will say their favorite day is any one spent during the week, at work, serving you. What a cunning siren song these folks sing, but they don't believe in their own lyrics. As always, it's just about sneaking on board for a free ride.

Are you comfortable with a defined role at work, or do you need to stretch yourself?
I'm not looking for a specific "right" answer to this question but, rather, some insight into the applicant's goals and interests. Has this individual worked as a loyal, dependable Crew Member for 10 years and is looking for a job that offers some growth? Is there a First Mate hiding inside, or perhaps someone with a taste for exploration or navigation?

The ones who bolt and run when faced with written job descriptions are the ones you don't want aboard.

A business needs Crew Members to do the majority of the work, but those in charge also need to groom the First Mates, Captains, Navigators, and Explorers of the future. This question opens the door for that small group of Crew Members who think past the 5:00 whistle. As Adam, the pressman from Chapter Six, did not understand, you never know where one step outside the comfortable little box of your job description will take you.

We cannot learn without listening, so if you're normally a big talker, the interview is the time to restrain yourself. Let the applicant lead the conversation to some extent. In addition to the above personality-specific queries, I have a number of general questions I work into interviews to gain some additional perspective:

What was your favorite job? What challenge are you most proud of having overcome? What are your goals for the next year, or for the next five years? How do you think you can help our business grow? What do you like most about living in this city?

I don't care as much about the specific answers to these general questions as I do about getting to know the applicant a little better. I try to imagine the person working with my crew and my customers and attempt to be as methodical as possible about my analysis. I know that carelessness and haste will haunt me later!

One final word of warning: Don't let the giddiness of hiring the "perfect" employee distract you from keeping your personnel files shipshape. The moment that new member of the crew steps aboard, hand over a written job description and employee manual. Even Radar couldn't actually read Colonel Blake's mind.... So don't expect the rest of the crew to know precisely what you want them to do without clarification.

I've learned that the ones who bolt and run when faced with written job descriptions are the ones you don't want aboard anyway. In addition to helping you down the road should any confusion arise over responsibilities, formal job descriptions serve as effective final screening tools.

As I wrote at the beginning of this book, no one goes into business to deal with people problems. Interviewing and hiring employees can be one of the most stressful aspects of any business owner's or manager's job. So, if you're struggling to assemble the ideal crew, resist the temptation to wax nostalgically about the good ol' days when it was just you: one person, one phone, one desk, and a clock radio. Wasn't life grand?

Well, let's bring that picture into slightly better focus: That one-man-band business was hardly a sturdy ship of commerce. It was more of a tippy little kayak. Any small swell in the stream demanded your full attention. And, while you focused on the small swell, you didn't see the rocks ahead. Lose the paddle, and you were dead. No "plan B," no life jacket.

With your new understanding of our six shipboard personalities, however, you now have some secure lifelines to hold fast to! By repeatedly practicing to identify the various personality types, you will eventually succeed in assembling the ideal crew.

Remember how, as a child, it took forever to learn to tie your shoelaces? "How do you make the big loop – is it on the left or on the right? How do you start the knot? And what do you do with the ends?" (Or, for the real-life sailors reading this, how difficult it was to master that most basic of knots, the bowline?) Today you don't even think about the process. Your management skills will soon be just as automatic.

CHAPTER NINE

Mutiny at Sea

Mutiny! The very word evokes images of violence and rebellion. From William Bligh of the *Bounty* to Jack Sparrow of *The Black Pearl*, captains real and fictitious have always faced the possibility of treachery on the high seas. Of course, with an able crew under your command and any Stowaways left behind at the dock, you probably feel you've got nothing but sunny skies ahead!

Sure, the daily race to stay ahead of the competition never abates, and every sailor worth his salt knows how economic swells can rock your ship…. But *you've* got a hardworking and loyal crew, capable of riding out any storm along the way to your goals.

Don't you?

The best story I've heard about a mutinous employee centered on a young man who appeared to have all the makings of a genuine First Mate. A computer programmer, Robert had joined the classified ad department at one of our country's largest newspapers to help install a new billing and reporting system. Energetic, smart, innovative, and always ready to lend less-experienced programmers a hand or pitch in after hours, Robert appeared the model worker. Brainstorming clever solutions for the latest challenge came naturally to him at the department's project meetings. If the project manager decided against using one of his suggestions, he'd nod agreeably and turn to the next person's idea. What an easy-going, smart guy, you'd have thought.

Well, it turned out Robert wasn't quite what he seemed. When the project manager rejected his ideas, he'd return to his desk and write the computer code for them anyway. Just imagine the domino effect of confusion one such rogue programmer could leave in his wake! The head-scratching on the part of his code-writing colleagues during in-house tests... the irritation among workers in other departments when they couldn't complete a simple operation that they'd had no problems with when using the old system...

Who knows how long the guy would have gotten away with his mischief had he not started bragging.

The nature of programming helped camouflage his mutinous actions. Programmers usually have several versions of their code accessible at a time while they do their own fine-tuning and testing. Say the project manager asked why So-and-So in accounts receivable couldn't run a test report. Robert would reply, "She wasn't supposed to use version X – that still has bugs in it. I told her to access *version Y*." By that time, the person in accounts receivable had moved on to something else, so the subject was moot. For several months, Robert got away with his subterfuge by pleasantly pointing the finger at everyone else.

And who knows how long the guy would have gotten away with his mischief had he not started bragging to his fellow programmers! Some began copying him, experimenting with unauthorized shortcuts or clever new ways of writing code. "If Robert can do it, why can't I? I'm as smart as he is!" In a sense, Robert was offering his co-workers a challenge, and while they probably didn't intend any harm to the project itself, the damage was done. Suddenly their work was a game and "If you can skirt the rules and get away with it, do!" their new motto.

With so much talk, word finally got to the boss. Fortunately, Robert was a contract worker, so the order to "walk the plank" needn't be preceded by progressive discipline. Even as he was escorted to the door, his co-workers were scrambling to clean up the mess left in his wake.

Not every employee problem is as dramatic as this rogue programmer. Yet good management requires dealing with *any* problem as swiftly as captains of yore sentenced troublemakers to a few trips 'round the keel.

I once hired a capable graphic designer named Susan. After about half a year on board, signs of trouble began floating to the surface. This once-efficient Crew Member began taking more and more time to complete her work. Then I noticed she quit bringing pen and paper to our initial meetings for new projects. She said she had no need for notes "because I can keep it all in my head." Later, when an error occurred, she conveniently claimed, "*Those details were never discussed.*"

About this time, Susan also started taking her breaks on a formal basis: 10 minutes precisely at 10:30 each morning, lunch from exactly 12:30 to 1:30, and an afternoon break at 2:30 on the dot. And, as their little circle's self-appointed leader, she insisted the three other female designers take their breaks with her (but none of the guys or other women on staff).

Now, employees in our industry typically take breaks on an informal basis. When you finish one task, take a few minutes for yourself before starting another. If a client calls, postpone your break for 10 minutes. This arrangement balances a designer's need for some creative rejuvenation time with our customers' expectations of good service. If the receptionist tried to put through a call from one of Susan's clients, however, she refused if it conflicted with her Official Break Time.

The realization I had a serious problem on my hands came the day Susan missed a project deadline. Her solution? "Call the client, and let him know it just isn't done." I reminded her that when you're in the business of designing, oh say, marketing materials for a promotional campaign, timeliness is critical. Meeting our deadlines is important, because clients have deadlines of their own.

From the look on her face, she was not getting the message. Perhaps she can relate to a more personal situation, I thought, and asked her to consider the following scenario: "You take your car in for service before work and are assured the work will be done by 5:00. How would you feel if you called the garage before returning to pick it up and were casually told it wouldn't be ready that day... that 'it would just take more time'"? Like an echo of Janet from Chapter Six, Susan responded to my hypothetical scenario with a dismissive, "That's *completely* different!"

As you see, Susan had changed her job title, demoting herself from dependable Crew Member to Stowaway.

So I did the only thing I could: I kept a close watch on her, documenting any transgressions for unprofessional behavior or violations of office rules. Within three weeks, I was able to let her go. Susan was shocked. I was none too pleased about the turn of events myself, but I knew in my heart that my only real option was to deal with her in a way that would make my customers happy.

The incident was an important reminder that a small problem is much easier to fix than a big one. The unhappy truth is that, while you're avoiding a minor personnel issue, it's only getting exponentially worse. Instead of a two-minute chat about the importance of taking notes, you face a 30-minute talk about the necessity of a flexible work schedule. Or that 30-minute meeting has blown up into a two-hour firestorm of emotion. If you let your customers' needs be your guide, you'll find it easier to dive in at the first sign of trouble.

Deferring confrontation will only prolong your misery and allow the curse of the Stowaway to spread.

Deferring confrontation will only prolong your misery and allow the curse of the Stowaway to spread as quickly as Robert the rogue programmer's mutiny did.

Marginal Crew Members will start bending the rules, perhaps even adopting some of the Stowaway's attitude themselves. Good First Mates will become dissatisfied. Navigators will wonder why no one cares about following their course plans for success and start looking for employment elsewhere. And when the Captain is also buddies with a mutinous crew, their ship may be springing leaks all around them without anyone taking notice.

I watched this happen at a local non-profit foundation a few years ago, when my firm was called in to assist with the creation of new marketing and fundraising materials.

After one or two meetings, I realized the foundation's marketing department consisted of two distinct groups of people: one productive, the other pretty darn useless. I dubbed this second group the "wallpaper workers." They hung around doing nothing, for all appearances just part of the decor. The wallpaper workers had been with the foundation for some time and were good pals with their Captain, the department manager. Show up in the morning, visit all day with friends, switch off the computer and head home at 5:00.... What more could a job possibly entail?!

Good Crew Members who are promoted beyond their capabilities can cause just as many headaches.

The productive workers, who'd come on board more recently, focused on the foundation's stated mission. These Crew Members concentrated on specific ways in which the new marketing materials could be used, on ideas for fundraising and awareness campaigns, on working within budget and scheduling constraints. The wallpaper workers and their clueless Captain cared only about calling more meetings. Oh, yes – and theorizing about what their pals who missed one meeting might have thought had they been present.

After some months of working with these folks, I watched as one after another of the productive employees grew dissatisfied and left. What hard-working Crew Member wants to stick around in such a frustrating environment? Yet with the Captain unwilling to manage her friends among the crew, the wallpaper workers felt snug and secure – oblivious to the fact they were engaged in a curious sort of self-destructive mutiny, a quiet and calm resistance movement against the foundation as a whole.

Their little ship finally ran aground when the fleet commander (in the form of the foundation's board of directors) fired them one and all. The money raised under their direction didn't even cover the cost of running the department. The wallpaper workers had unconsciously conspired to undermine their department – and through it, the foundation's mission – while their Captain sat back and let it happen. Too busy acting as their friend, the Captain forgot her duty as their leader.

Good Crew Members who are promoted beyond their capabilities can cause just as many headaches as those who think they can float along as Stowaways forever, like the non-profit foundation's oddly mutinous crew. Con sider a former employee of mine named Mike.

A talented and dependable First Mate, Mike had worked with me for more than six years, and I was starting to move him up the ladder in responsibility and pay. Then his wife lost her job, and his family hit a difficult financial patch. Encouraged by his wife, Mike expressed a desire to assume a more senior role at the firm. We sat down to put his new responsibilities and corresponding salary in writing. Everything looked fine on paper – except Mike thought he and a buddy could "be in charge together," sharing the responsibility of overseeing the support staff and handling client-management tasks. I questioned whether our little ship (we only employed seven workers at the time) had room for three Captains. Still, Mike was a valued member of the crew, so I thought I'd give it a try.

Reliance on your gut instincts can be invaluable in such cases. I was sure our business would be "over-captained," yet I agreed to Mike's idea. I thought he deserved a reward for his years of loyal work, so I did the "nice" thing. A good Captain may not always go with his gut instinct, but he should acknowledge his instinct and have a good reason for setting it aside. As you'll see, my reason wasn't good enough....

We enjoyed fair skies for a few months. Then Mike's buddy walked in one morning and gave me his notice; he was leaving the firm to pursue other opportunities. Mike was shattered. He couldn't fathom being in charge without his friend's support.

I realized Mike had never really aspired to being a Captain; he just needed the money. How often eager Crew Members see the prestige and privileges of a promotion, while turning a blind eye to the responsibilities, the potential stress, and the time commitment of a more senior position.

Two weeks later – on the first day of work without his buddy – Mike handed in his notice, too. I was sorry to lose him. Mike was a great First Mate but a poor Captain.

Had I persuaded Mike to continue in a role he was obviously unfit for, the situation might have eventually bred resentment on his part that could have permeated through our small crew. Keeping an unhappy worker around – even as an act of supposed kindness – can still poison morale, lead to poor productivity and general dissatisfaction, and eventually turn a crew against those in charge.

In fact, resentment among Crew Members can prove as damaging to a business leader's authority, and to the business itself, as wood rot on a boat. And it really doesn't matter whether that resentment is justified or not. Just think about the problems that arise at promotion time.

The president of a large commercial printer in my city once shared with me his own such experience. Curt's shop employed more than 60 workers, including three full-time delivery drivers. Two of the drivers had been with the printer for more than 10 years; the third, much younger, had been with the company less than half that time. The difference in work styles between the drivers couldn't have been more pronounced: The senior men lounged at the loading dock smoking cigarettes when they had free time between deliveries, while the younger guy swept out his truck and helped out in the shop.

> **A Captain may not always go with his gut instinct, but he should have a good reason for setting it aside.**

As his business grew, my friend decided he needed someone to manage his delivery and shipping operations. He chose the younger driver. You can imagine the senior drivers' incensed reaction: "We've been here for 10 years – how could you overlook us? *One of us deserves this job!*"

Curt explained to them he was looking for a go-getter, someone who would do more than he was asked to do. Someone like the younger man. Begrudgingly, they accepted the reasoning behind his decision. After all, each had the job he truly wanted: driving around town and smoking cigarettes.

Had my friend backed down, he would have sent a message as loud as a foghorn to the junior driver and every other go-getter at the company: Don't work too hard. Seniority, not actual skills and extra effort, earn you promotions and pay raises around here. Their resentment would have been understandable. No doubt, most would've eventually found employment elsewhere. And I'd bet that any good workers who stuck around would have ended up just average employees. After all, festering resentment only fuels disloyalty to a Captain and his ship.

The unjustified resentment of the senior drivers was just as potentially destructive, of course. Fortunately, my friend was able to diffuse the situation with some straight talking. Most people see the impact of a decision from their own perspectives. How does this affect *me*? They don't usually think about how a decision impacts the business's customers, or the competition. As Curt knew, a few minutes spent sharing the thought process that went into a decision is often enough to dispel bad feelings and misunderstandings.

The bottom line is that if resolving a personnel situation will improve your customers' lives, you'd better do it. An able Captain doesn't head below deck for a nap when the radar indicates a storm on approach! Grab hold of the rigging.... Stay your course.... This storm too shall pass!

CHAPTER TEN

Land Ho!

One hand for the boat, the other for you. The first rule taught to every novice sailor developed from centuries of hapless accidents at sea. A sudden swell, a slippery deck, the boom swinging around when least expected... you never know what's waiting to knock you off your feet. A simple safety precaution – always keep hold of something solid as you move about the boat – can prevent an embarrassing stumble from turning into a dangerous fall overboard.

Life on board your ship of commerce is no different. You can't control how the business world tosses your little vessel around, or how many conniving Stowaways lurk in every port. You can control how well prepared you are, and how you react to the stormier situations you encounter far from the safety of shore.

Understanding how to identify and manage the six shipboard characters you've met in the preceding pages is central to exerting that control over the direction your business, and your life, takes you.

No matter how seaworthy you think you are, though, life certainly has a way of keeping things exciting. Although I laugh about it today, one of my fondest memories of a challenging Crew Member was more frustrating than amusing at the time.

I once employed a young woman named Angela as our office manager. Her responsibilities included answering the phones, light bookkeeping, proofreading, and generally lending a hand wherever needed. Most people have interests outside of work, and one of Angela's was a passion for Italy and all things Italian. As a firm believer that education ought to be a lifelong endeavor, I always applaud my employees' efforts to find new opportunities for growth. So when Angela mentioned she was starting to study Italian, I told her I thought it was a great idea. Her efforts at self-improvement soon took an unexpected turn, however....

> **Angela had decorated her work area with photographs of desk chairs cut from an office-supply catalog.**

One day, while looking through a filing cabinet, I noticed new file tabs on the manila folders. Where I was used to seeing such words as *invoices*, *employee*, and *equipment*, I now saw *fatture*, *impiegata*, and *apparecchiatura*. I continued combing through the files and noticed that the monthly folders now read *gennaio* and *febbraio* instead of *January* and *February*.

Angela had relabeled all our files in Italian.

Highly pleased with her ingenious system, Angela explained that it would help with her language lessons. Great. I'm no longer in the graphic design business – I'm running a language school! I took a deep breath and prayed, "Dear God, give me patience!"

I sat Angela down for a little chat about the effect of her new classification system on our business overall. I began by saying how much I understood her interest in the country of her forefathers. I repeated my belief that learning a new language is a wonderful project. However, I added with emphasis, the new system was not helping us help our clients, nor did it streamline office operations (to say the least). Angela only spoke a little Italian, I gently pointed out, and the rest of the crew's Italian was limited to pizza, manicotti, and Fiat. The new system had to go – *rapidamente.* She switched the labels back and all went well, for a time....

A month or so later, Angela started to complain of back trouble. I asked when she first noticed the pain. About the time she began taking modern dance lessons, it turns out. Upon further inquiry, I learned that the group practiced every night from 9:00 until midnight and that her dances involved rolling around on her back on a hardwood floor. Hmmm... dance lessons... rolling around on the floor... sore back. Could this be a pattern?

Oh, no! Angela insisted her office chair was to blame. I pointed out that we all used similar chairs, that they were fairly new, and that her physical ailment only manifested itself after she began rolling around on her back after hours. These attempts at reasoning merely resulted in a small standoff. Then, several mornings later, I walked in to discover that Angela had decorated her work area with a dozen or so photographs of desk chairs cut from an office-supply catalog. "Keep breathing," I said to myself!

"My mother told me to visualize anything I need," she explained patiently, "and if I have pictures of what I need, it will increase the chance of making my vision come true." I told her that the exercise of her new "craft" in the office was inappropriate. I suggested she move the photography exhibit to her home, where she could focus on her vision more effectively.

I truly liked Angela. She was a sweet person – but she had a difficult time separating her personal life from work. Within six months, Angela had moved on to a new job. I do miss her, sort of.

Whether you're dealing with an Angela, or someone more dangerous like the code-writing mutineer from Chapter Nine, resist the urge to cry "Mayday!" Tell yourself instead that the rough times usually teach us more about effective management – and about ourselves – than all the sunny days just spent coasting along.

After all, these six shipboard characters pertain to you, too. Of course, I don't know whether you're a Navigator or a First Mate or a Crew Member eager to expand your horizons, but you will. Gaining insight into yourself is just as valuable as understanding who your crewmates are.

As you've made your way through these pages, you might have found yourself identifying with a personality type you don't really care for. That's okay! What you are now may influence your future, but it does not define it. Just as the lessons in this book will help you set a new course for your business by better identifying those people around you, they can help you set a new course in your personal development, too.

LAND HO!

If the ship you're sailing on is your own, congratulate yourself when things go well. When you make a successful crossing, recognize it as such and thank the Crew Members who helped you reach that distant port safely. Ask yourself whether the voyage was a profitable one overall, one that you want to repeat and that your customers actually need. Consider also whether you should make any changes before the next trip. Do you need a First Mate, a Navigator, additional Crew Members? Have you discovered a Stowaway or two?

If you work on the crew of someone else's ship, are you comfortable in your current role? Are you fulfilled? Every business needs many types of people to succeed. Explorers, Navigators, Captains, First Mates, and Crew Members are each valuable in their own way. It is important to think about which of these personality types best describes you today, and how you feel about yourself in that role. If you're not comfortable, or feel it's time to reach for new heights, today is the day to begin! Change is scary, and not without risk – but only you can make the investment in yourself to bring about a happier and more fulfilling future.

You might have found yourself identifying with a personality type you don't care for. That's okay!

Change is even more difficult for Stowaways. You've relied on your wits for so long that an honest assessment of your life is often too much of a hassle. But sooner or later you will crash. Many times Stowaways start to rely on alcohol, drugs, or dysfunctional relationships. Yet as Shackleton learned, even Stowaways can become valuable members of a crew. "It is never too late to be what you might have been," George Eliot once said.

When I consider my own shipboard personality, I want (vainly) to pick one of the more prestigious roles: a 100% heroic, swashbuckling Explorer, perhaps. To be honest, however, I must admit I'm more of a blended type: about 50% Navigator, 20% Explorer, and 30% Captain.

My Navigator persona is the puzzle-solver. He understands where my clients are headed and is excited by the process of gathering resources and brainstorming concepts to speed them on their way.

My Explorer side is highly creative and clever. He enjoys a dynamic work environment and the challenge of new ventures, such as taking on a client in an unfamiliar industry or writing this book.

The Captain job falls to me by default. I spend a good deal of time in my Captain shoes simply because my business needs me in that role. Most of this time, I am a dependable leader, with a strong sense of duty to both clients and crew. But, I'm also human. After particularly difficult work periods, I find myself staring out the window wondering if I really want to be here.

Take a moment to reflect on the great variety of riches that should be accumulating in your ship's hold.

At times like that, I've learned it's okay to adopt just a little of the Stowaway's attitude and escape below deck! Turn your back on work for an hour, an afternoon, a weekend. Immerse yourself in the people and activities that fill you up rather than drain you. Pretending I don't have a business-related care in the world, for a time, rejuvenates me enough that I return to the office with renewed appreciation of my job's diverse aspects and interesting challenges.

LAND HO!

I'm sure you've realized that our nautical analogy of a ship crossing the sea to a distant port applies to life in general, not just the world of business! At the end of their decades-long careers, most people don't even mention the money they've earned or material goods they've acquired. They speak with pride of the things they've built, the people they've worked with and friendships they've formed, the contributions they've made to their field, to their community, or to society. Those who recognize such invaluable inner riches are the truly wealthy ones.

As we reach the end of our journey together and cry "Land ho!", take a moment to reflect on the great variety of riches that should be accumulating in your ship's hold: the pleasure in jobs well done, the satisfaction of providing quality services or products that others need, the enjoyment of a business environment that allows everyone on the crew to balance work and family life.... If you find yourself weighted down with less valuable cargo, it's time to re-evaluate where you're headed and who's on board!

This wonderful, wide world of ours offers too many opportunities for exploration to sit in port lamenting our business woes, much less our lot in life. You are now well-qualified to gather up an able crew and set your sights on new shores. Today is the day to start making your life a wonderful experience. I wish you a safe journey – and Godspeed!

Index

attire 89-90, 90-91
AutoNation 21-22

Banting, Frederick and
  Best, Charles 27
Blackborow, Perce 85-86, 87
Bligh, Captain William 103
BLOCKBUSTER 21-22

Callaway Golf 17
Captains 15, 18, 41-50, 51,
  53, 118
  characteristics of 41-47
  identification of 45-46
  interviewing for 97-98
  management of 48-50
  notable examples of:
    Welch, Jack 43, 50
  and relationship with
  First Mate 53
  suggestions for 50
  talents and drawbacks 44
change, fear of 40, *see also*
  motivation
Chevrolet 17
communication
  with customers 50
  with employees 49, 52-
  53, 67-68, 107
Crew Members 15, 63-74
  characteristics of 63-66
  interviewing for 99-100
  management of 66-73
  suggestions for 73-74
  talents and drawbacks 69
customers, needs of 17, 26,
  71, 90, 112

del Cano, Juan Sebastian
  21, 33
Diebold, Charles 25
Diebold Safe & Lock Co.
  25-26

Eliot, George 117
employees, *see also* interviews
  and appropriate attire 89-
  90, 90-91
  conflicts between 61-62
  difficulties identifying 14,
  102
  and feeling threatened by
  Explorers 23-24
  and job descriptions 36,
  48, 67, 101
  and motives for working
  14, 23, 63-64, 72, 73-74
  and their perceptions 28-
  29, 53, 64-66, 70-72, 112
  training of 15, 47
  and terminations 84, 107
  and turnover 38, 49
  vs. employers 11-12

INDEX

Explorers 15, 19-30, 51, 118
  characteristics of 19-25
  identification of 21-25
  interviewing for 95
  management of 26-30
  notable examples of:
    Banting, Frederick and
    Best, Charles 27; Diebold,
    Charles 25; Huizenga,
    Wayne 21-22, 30; Magellan, Ferdinand 20-21, 26,
    30; McDonald, Dick and
    Mac 32-33
  and their relationship
    with Navigators 21, 31,
    33-34, 39-40, 87
  suggestions for 30
  talents and drawbacks 28
Extended Stay America 22

First Mates 15, 51-62
  characteristics of 51-59
  identification of 59-60
  interviewing for 98-99
  management of 60-61
  notable examples of:
    Radar 53, 101
  and their relationship
    with Captains 53, 55-56
  suggestions for 61-62
  talents and drawbacks 57
Ford, Henry 34, 36-37

General Electric Co. 43
General Nutrition Cntrs. 17

hiring, *see* interviews
Huizenga, Wayne 21-22, 30

IBM 88
interviews 14, 88-89, 91-101
  and appropriate attire 89-90, 90-91
  and catching potential
    Stowaways 76, 79, 83, 90-92
  and hiring mistakes 13-14, 93
  questions for 95-101
  strategies for 93-94

job descriptions 36, 48, 67, 101

Kroc, Ray 33

lottery 30, 73-74, *see also*
  motivation

M*A*S*H 53
Magellan, Ferdinand 20-21, 26, 30
management
  of Captains 48-50
  and communication problems 49
  of Crew Members 66-73
  and delegation 45-46
  effective examples of 12, 42, 50

INDEX

of Explorers 26-30
of First Mates 60-61
and handling of Stowaways 84, 87
and hiring mistakes 13-14, 93
and ineffectiveness 55-56, 66-67
and lessons of adversity 18
of Navigators 38
techniques for 12
and training, lack of 12
McDonald, Dick and Mac 32-33
MGM Mirage 17
Miami Dolphins 30
motivation
  to change 30, 84-85, 86, 117, 119
  to work 11, 14, 23, 63-64, 72, 73-74, 119
mutiny
  and effects on crew 105, 107-108, 109, 110-111
  examples of 103-105, 105-107, 108-109, 109-110
  prevention of 111-112

Navigators 15, 31-40, 51, 118
  characteristics of 31-37
  identification of 37-38
  interviewing for 96-97
  management of 38

  notable examples of:
    Anson, Commodore George 32; del Cano, Juan Sebastian 21, 33; Ford, Henry 34, 36-37; Kroc, Ray 33; Schultz, Howard 40
  and their relationship with Explorers 21, 31, 33-34, 39-40, 87
  suggestions for 39-40
  talents and drawbacks 37

promotions and raises 65-70, 110-112

raises 80-81, *see also* promotions and raises
risk, acceptance of 20, 25, 73

San Diego Zoo 17
Schultz, Howard 40
Segway Human Transporter 32
Shackleton, Sir Ernest 85-86, 117
Sparrow, Captain Jack 103
Sony 17
Star Trek 35
Starbucks 40, 71
Stowaways 15, 16, 18, 75-86, 118
  characteristics of 75-77
  and effects on crew 85

examples of 76, 77-78, 79-81, 82-83, 90-91, 105-107
liberation from 84, 87
notable examples of: Blackborow, Perce 85-86, 87
reformation of 77, 84-85, 86, 87
suggestions for 86
talents and drawbacks 82
warning signs of 78, 79, 83, 88-89, 91-92, 100

Target 40
terminations 84, 107
training 12, 15, 47
turnover 38, 49

Viacom 22
vitality curve 43

Waste Management 21-22
Wells Fargo Bank 25